SCENES FROM
CANADIAN PLAYS
SINCE 1990

PURE GOLD

Scenes from Canadian Plays since 1990

Edited by Brian Kennedy

PLAYWRIGHTS CANADA PRESS
TORONTO • CANADA

Playwrights Canada Press
The Canadian Drama Publisher
215 Spadina Ave., Suite 230, Toronto, Ontario, Canada M5T 2C7
phone 416.703.0013 fax 416.408.3402
orders@playwrightscanada.com • www.playwrightscanada.com

For professional or amateur production rights, please contact
Playwrights Canada Press at the address above.

The publisher acknowledges the support of the Canadian taxpayers through the Government
of Canada Book Publishing Industry Development Program, the Canada Council for the Arts,
the Ontario Arts Council, and the Ontario Media Development Corporation.

Cover images © copyright Jupiterimages
Cover Design: Blake Sproule
Production Editor: Micheline Courtemanche

Library and Archives Canada Cataloguing in Publication

Pure gold : scenes from Canadian plays
since 1990 / edited by Brian Kennedy.

ISBN 978-0-88754-910-6

1. Canadian drama (English)--20th century.
2. Canadian drama (English)--21st century.
I. Kennedy, Brian, 1951-

PS8307.P87 2010   C812.008   C2009-907049-9

First edition: February 2010
Printed and bound in Canada by Gauvin Press, Gatineau

To Angela Rebeiro,
for a career devoted to the promotion
of many of these fine Canadian playwrights
and a wealth of others.

CONTENTS

Part Four: Scenes for More

INTRODUCTION

This selection of scenes is intended as an introduction to the most recent generation of Canadian playwrights and their award-winning works since 1990. It serves also as an updated version of the very successful collection, *You're Making A Scene* (Playwrights Canada Press, 1993), an anthology which drew from earlier decades.

Significantly, a large majority of dramatists in *Pure Gold* are second- or even third-generation professional, Canadian playwrights. All but two are born between the years 1948 and 1968; many attend Montreal's National Theatre School or graduate with BFAs from Canadian universities in the seventies or eighties; most join or found theatre companies, starting professional careers as actors, directors, playwrights—or, more commonly, juggle all three creative tasks. By the final decade of the century, these artists are Canada's writers, actors, directors, and professors of experience and vision, typically with several Governor General's Literary Awards, Dora Mavor Moore Awards, Floyd S. Chalmers Canadian Play Awards, Jessie Richardson Theatre Awards, or other provincial drama awards to prove it.[1]

The introductions to individual scenes in this anthology attempt to illuminate in a small way this unique cultural demographic. As a generation, they stand on the broad shoulders of theatrical innovators like Michel Tremblay, David French, and George F. Walker, to name a few, who are responsible for the remarkable Canadian theatrical renaissance of the early seventies, and who themselves owe a great debt of independence to our first generation of post-war professional playwrights, Gratien Gélinas and Marcel Dubé, Gwen Pharis Ringwood, Robertson Davies, and others.

This first post-war generation was by no means the initial stage of the Canadian theatre history. These traditions stretched back to the military garrisons of pre-Confederation times.[2] Yet the post-war generation was a unique departure from the largely colonial drama of the Little Theatre era (with some notable exceptions).[3] Theatre in the 1950s began to support full-time professionals, aided by the financial rewards of radio and television writing. These artists were encouraged and supported (albeit indirectly) by the publication of the Massey-Lévesque Report (1951) and the subsequent government funding for culture through the creation of the Canada Council for the Arts, which represented a seminal acknowledgement of the place of the arts in the national vision of all Canadians. Together with the CBC (itself inspired by another pro-culture, royal report, the Aird Commission of 1929) and a renewed sense of nationalism post-1967, government funding transformed the strictly amateur roles of the "little theatres" of the pre-war Dominion into full-time jobs. Theatre positions in the National Arts Centre, the National Theatre School, the Stratford and Shaw Festivals, regional theatres, alternative theatres, and post-secondary fine arts programs turned a pastime into a profession in Canada. Coincidentally, professional theatre in Canada came of age during the decades when the playwrights of this anthology were being born.

Thus, *Pure Gold*'s well-crafted scenes are by career playwrights who have fulfilled the ideals and are the beneficiaries of earlier dreams. Dramas, in both English and French, demonstrate a mastery of style and a fluency of dramatic language—a strong, resilient alloy that can only be forged by a life in the theatre within a nation that supports a living theatre culture.

Generally, these playwrights distinguish themselves from the previous generations of Canadian dramatists in several ways. First, by the immense variety of their subject matter, unburdened by nationalist fervour or one political point of view. Plays are set within the dark wonderland of imagination, like Morris Panych's *Girl in the Goldfish Bowl*, or are grounded in physicality and timed to the rhythms of farce, as in Allan Stratton's satire, *The Phoenix Lottery*. Others portray the struggle that is the heart of all great drama, as in Andrew Moodie's compelling biographic portrait, *The Real McCoy*, where genius battles the institutional racism of the early twentieth century.

Secondly, these playwrights are distinguished by the versatility of their own talent: many are successful actors and directors of stage, film, and television as well as writers of scripts and screenplays. Thus, they have collected as many Genies as the Chalmers, Doras, and Governor General's Literary Awards that adorn their mantles.

Thirdly, although there are still far too few plays translated from French to English and vice versa, Canada's two solitudes do seem to be slightly more aware of one another's accomplishments now than in the past. Through the efforts of translators such as Linda Gaboriau, who has produced over sixty translations of French plays and won both a Governor General's Literary Award and a Dora Mavor Moore Award in the process, and John Murrell, himself a successful playwright and recent recipient of the Governor General's Lifetime Artistic Achievement Award, and their publishers, Canadians can read excellent translations of some national award-winning plays, such as the scenes included in this volume by Carole Fréchette, Daniel Danis, Michel Marc Bouchard, and Wajdi Mouawad. Surely there is room for more funding in this area over the next decade.

Lastly, it may also be possible to divine the broad outlines of a national culture in these works and hear what flows beneath the surface of our country, and always has: from the loud, destructive rushing of Canada's wars, whether the Great War (Kerr, Thiessen, Massicotte), the Cold War (Sherman), or more recent conflicts (MacLeod, Mouawad, Fréchette, Wagner); to the dams of alienation, either through poverty (Banks, Danis, Stetson), family (Mighton, Panych, Thompson, Stratton), race (Sears, Moodie), or gender (Pollock, Murphy, Bouchard); and finally, to a few deep, satisfying draughts of Shakespeare (Findley, MacDonald). It is hoped these twenty-five excerpts, limited only by length, will still allow the careful reader to sense these strong, persistent undercurrents of our national literature.

Brian Kennedy

NOTES

1 Since 1937, the Governor General's Literary Awards (the GGs) have been given annually to the best books over several categories, in English and in French. Other drama awards mentioned in this volume are in nature more regional, such as Vancouver's Jessie Richardson (Jessie) and Toronto's Dora Mavor Moore (Dora), or the Alberta Playwriting Competition. The Genie Awards are given annually by the Academy of Canadian Cinema and Television.

2 Brian Kennedy, *The Baron Bold and the Beauteous Maid* (Toronto: Playwrights Canada Press, 2005).

3 Ibid., Ch. 3.

PART ONE

Scenes for Two

Joan MacLeod (1954–)

AMIGO'S BLUE GUITAR

1M / 1F

Joan MacLeod was born in 1954 in Vancouver. She joined Toronto's Tarragon Theatre in 1985 as playwright-in-residence. Over the next six years, she wrote and premiered her three most widely known works to date: *Toronto, Mississippi* (1987), *Amigo's Blue Guitar* (1990), and *The Hope Slide* (1992). In 1992, MacLeod returned to British Columbia to work with Vancouver's award-winning Green Thumb Theatre, recognized for its socially conscious Theatre for Young Audiences, or TYA drama. MacLeod's significant contribution was *The Shape of a Girl*, a play that dealt with the issue of teen bullying.

Originally, Joan MacLeod began writing poetry, as the memorable imagery and aural nuances of her plays attest. The central image of this 1990 play is Kitty Wells's country song, "Amigo's Blue Guitar," a metaphor for Elias's struggle to regain his dignity from a tortured past in El Salvador. Ironically, the sponsoring family has issues of their own. The father, Owen, sees a reminder in Elias of his own past as a Vietnam draft dodger; his son, Sander (nineteen), sees Elias as his attempt to succeed in his own faltering academic life; his daughter, Callie (twenty), falls in love with Elias—or at least with his horrific past—and further complicates his life by taking him to her bed. Scene four of the second act exposes their fated relationship for what it is and exemplifies MacLeod's skill at juggling both emotional and political themes at once.

MacLeod's Governor General's Literary Award was for *Amigo's Blue Guitar* in 1991. She has also won the Chalmers Award for *The Hope Slide*. Her plays have been produced across Canada and translated into five languages.

Interior, six weeks later. CALLIE and ELIAS in bed.

CALLIE	Do you ever dream you can't speak? Maybe I'm with Dad on the boat and something really terrible will happen if I can't warn him. But my throat is full of concrete. Only little noises come out, like a bird.
ELIAS	I do not dream.
CALLIE	That's because you never sleep…
ELIAS	And that, Callie, is because you will not let me. Always you are coming to my room.
CALLIE	Tell me not to.
ELIAS	This is a hard thing.
CALLIE	Exactly. It's snowing again. Snow in April.
ELIAS	I like the snow.
CALLIE	Coming in from the north. Maybe it will travel all the way to El Salvador. Big clouds of snow.
ELIAS	I don't think so.
CALLIE	It'll cover up the cities, the mountains…
ELIAS	We do never have snow in Salvador.
CALLIE	The layers of ash…. What scares you more than anything?
ELIAS	Many things have scared me.
CALLIE	The most scared you've been, ever.
ELIAS	When I hear the knock on the door, softly…
CALLIE	Yes.
ELIAS	And there you are, back in my room.
CALLIE	I'm serious.
ELIAS	And I wish to talk of the snow.

CALLIE	Will you miss me?
ELIAS	Yes, of course.
CALLIE	I miss you already. Only three more days. I wish you weren't going.
ELIAS	This is a good thing, working on your father's boat.
CALLIE	Yeah, well, just wait until you've been cooped up out there for a month with Dad and a bunch of dead fish.
ELIAS	We do not kill the fish.
CALLIE	Dead or alive they all stink and Dad's a pain in the ass.
ELIAS	And what scares you the most?
CALLIE	More than anything?
ELIAS	Yes.
CALLIE	Drunk people. People so pissed their eyes roll back in their head and you can't, you know, reason with them.
ELIAS	You have drunk people in your family?
CALLIE	No, no… just guys I've gone out with, that sort of thing.
ELIAS	Yes, you do have many boyfriends.
CALLIE	No I don't.
ELIAS	Pretend the drunk man you are afraid of is under the bed, or behind the door, is there in your room, always.
CALLIE	That's terrible.
ELIAS	And when you close your eyes he is there also. He never goes away, ever.
CALLIE	The people that put you in prison, they…
ELIAS	No. I am talking about a different thing. I am talking about a big fear in my country that you would not know of.
CALLIE	But I want to know. How can I understand the things that have happened to you if you won't tell me?
ELIAS	They are good things to leave behind.

CALLIE	Look at your scars. They're whiter at night, nearly silver…
ELIAS	*Plateado, enfermedad, pox.*
CALLIE	Bullshit.
ELIAS	No shit, Canada is all right… *avion plateado.*
CALLIE	The silver airplane.
ELIAS	In my prison there is an old kitchen. On the ceiling, a silver wheel with a rope… una maquina… *[a machine…]*
CALLIE	A winch.
ELIAS	We are taken to this room to wait for the *avion plateado.* When the guard comes, my brother's hands are put behind his back and legs and like this he is hung from the winch. *Avion plateado.* It is my brother that is the silver airplane…
CALLIE	But you said…
ELIAS	And the guard asks him, do you wish to fly with or without a *piloto…*
CALLIE	A pilot.
ELIAS	"Without," he says. He swings my brother so hard his head is hit and hit and hit and hit into the wall and he tells him an airplane that flies without a pilot always will… *choquar…* *(makes a crashing sound)*
CALLIE	Crash…
ELIAS	By the time it is dark he has finished breathing. Then it is my turn. I cry that I wish to fly with a pilot. The guard laughs: "*Yo soy el piloto*—I am the pilot." The guard climbs onto my back. My arms break. My skin opens. My eyes close.
CALLIE	*(pause)* I am sorry.
ELIAS	This is my story. What is it you wish to do with it now?
CALLIE	To… I don't know.
ELIAS	What? This is the thing you have been wanting. No?
CALLIE	Let me hold you.

ELIAS   This is not what I wish.

CALLIE   Your other brother. Is he in danger, too?

ELIAS   Everyone is in danger.

CALLIE   Let me help them, or…

ELIAS   *Eso es imposible.*

CALLIE   Then let me help you forget.

ELIAS   This is not a true thing you are wanting.

CALLIE   I love you.

ELIAS   No, Callie.

CALLIE   Yes, I do.

ELIAS   You love these terrible things that I remember.

Colleen Wagner (1949–)

THE MONUMENT

1M / 1F

Colleen Wagner is a playwright, screenwriter, and actor born in Alberta who now teaches at York University in Toronto. Her first play, *Sand* (Nightwood Theatre, 1986), was nominated for best international play at The Royal Exchange Theatre in Manchester, England. It was her third play, *The Monument* (1995), after being nominated for a Dora and winning the GG Award in 1996, that gained her an international reputation. *The Monument* has been staged around the world; indeed, it has the distinction of being the first commercially produced Canadian play in China. Wagner is working on a screenplay of this work.

The Monument is a raw, unsettling two-hander that confronts the brutality of the Bosnian war of the early 1990s and the suspension of humanity during any war. Its two characters are Stetko, a nineteen-year-old soldier sentenced to death for war crimes, and Mejra, a fifty-year-old mother whose daughter is among those raped and murdered by Stetko during the conflict. The play opens with Stetko strapped to the electric chair, about to die for war crimes.

Presumably because Mejra has been so victimized by the war, she is permitted to offer Stetko a commutation—only if he agrees "to do as she says for the rest of his life." Of course, he agrees, but soon realizes that her plan is to teach him the difference between the truth and lies, good and evil, in as vengeful a way as possible. Finally, he brings her to the graves of her daughter and the other twenty-two women he raped and murdered during the war. Here, she forces him to dig up their bodies with his bare hands, forces him to remember each death as he slowly piles their unearthed and mutilated corpses to build a macabre monument to his brutality.

In this scene, just after his release, Mejra has yoked Stetko, like an ox, to a plough that she directs. The plough has hit a rock and Mejra seizes the opportunity to begin Stetko's rehabilitation.

MEJRA swiftly unhooks him from the yoke, cuffs his hands in front, and drags him by his chains to the rock.

MEJRA   Dig it out.

STETKO   How?

MEJRA   With your feet. Your mouth. Your nose.
I don't care.
Just do it.

> *STETKO assesses the rock for a moment then proceeds to poke with one foot. He whistles a long note.*

STETKO   She's a big one.

MEJRA   Dig.

> *He works harder, using both feet. This motion develops into a kind of Russian jig or march. He sings and kicks at the dirt until he tires.*

STETKO   This is sunstroke weather.

MEJRA   For idiots, yes.

STETKO   What's life, eh?
Drudgery, and a few dances in between.
Care to dance, madam?

MEJRA   Dig.

STETKO   Take off my shirt.

It's hot.

I like the sun.
I never saw daylight in prison.
It's the first hot day of the year.

> *MEJRA strikes him.*

MEJRA   Stinko, you are nothing.
No one.

                    A dog.
                    A slave.
                    A murderer.

STETKO   I know what I am.
                    I know I'm a murderer
                    and a dog
                    and a slave.
                    I don't care.
                    I'm not proud.
                    I can be those things.

MEJRA   You are those things.

STETKO   So what?
                    So what do we do with that?
                    Kill me?
                    You went to a lot of trouble to save me.
                    Why? Eh?
                    What do you want?
                    I'm your dog and slave.
                    I'm Stinko the murderer.
                    So what?

                         MEJRA sits on the rock.

MEJRA   So what?
                    Right.
                    So what.
                    What do we do with dogs and slaves and murderers?

                    What would you do?

STETKO   Shoot them, probably.

MEJRA   Shoot them.

STETKO   Yeah.
                    It's simple.

MEJRA   Maybe I should shoot you.

STETKO   You like me.

MEJRA   Understand one thing if you can, stupido—I despise you.

STETKO   So shoot me.

Silence.

So use me like a dog and a slave till it's time to shoot me.
Do you think I care? Eh?
What do I have to care about?

MEJRA   Don't look for pity!
Dig!

Pause.

*He begins, furious at first, then grins and switches again
to his manic dance, singing at the top of his lungs, kicking
dirt everywhere until the rock is exposed. He clasps his
handcuffed arms around the boulder and heaves with all his
might and lifts the rock triumphantly to his chest. He turns
as if he would hurl the rock at her, but it's impossible.*

Go ahead.
Show me what you're really made of.
Smash my face with it.

STETKO laughs at his own impotence.

Drop it on your foot.

STETKO   *(suddenly serious)* I can't.

MEJRA   Why not?

STETKO   I don't know.

MEJRA puts her foot beneath the rock.

MEJRA   Drop it on mine.

*He releases the rock immediately. She pulls her foot away
in time.*

Try again.

STETKO   *(laughs)* It's too heavy.

MEJRA   Pick it up.

STETKO   You are one strange woman.

MEJRA   Who are you to judge?
Pick it up.

> *STETKO attempts to pick it up but can't.*

STETKO   Impossible.

MEJRA   A moment ago it was possible.
Pick it up or I'll bury you in this field.

STETKO   I can't pick it up now.
I had strength then.
I don't now.
I used it all up.
Who do you think I am—Hercules? I can lift mountains
on command?

MEJRA   Didn't you kill on command?

> *No response.*

Which is harder? Killing someone or lifting a mountain?
Is that where your strength is, Stinko?
In hatred?
If you hate enough you can lift a mountain and kill a people,
on command.

STETKO   I don't hate them.

MEJRA   You kill people you like?

> *Silence.*

Learn to hate me, Stinko, because you are going to lift that rock
on command or be buried alive in this field.

STETKO   I wish you'd never come to save me.

MEJRA   I never came to save you.

STETKO   You said you were my saviour.

MEJRA   I lied.

You know all about lies, don't you?
Haven't you ever said to a young girl, I'll show you the forest.

STETKO   I never!

MEJRA   Someday you'll take me to this forest.

STETKO   What do you mean?

MEJRA   You look nervous.
We all know about the forest.
Dead bodies.
Not your girlfriend though.
She died on the street.
A virgin.

> *STETKO weeps.*

You're right, Stetko.
I am your saviour.

Now pick up that rock because you owe me.
Pick it up out of gratitude instead of hate.

Go on.

> *He tries, but in vain.*

Hate works best for you.

STETKO   For you, too.
You hate me.

MEJRA   Yes.

STETKO   Why?

MEJRA   I might kill you before I could finish my sentence.

> *Pause.*

STETKO   You're one of "them," aren't you?

MEJRA   What if I am?

STETKO   My aunt is one.
My father's brother married one.
I used to see them a lot.
Before.

Now everybody fights.
The whole family.

Everyone thinks they're right.
That's why people need someone to take charge.
Keep people in line. Make them shut up and do as they're told.

MEJRA   You?

STETKO   Not me
but somebody.

MEJRA   Then you'll like our arrangement.
It's a dictatorship.
I'm the dictator.
I tell you what to do and you do it.

STETKO   Sure.
I don't care.
People don't care who's in charge just so long as they don't
have to take responsibility.

MEJRA   I'll take responsibility.
Pick up the rock and drop it on your foot.

STETKO   It's not normal to injure yourself.

MEJRA   It's normal to harm someone else?

STETKO   I've done nothing to you.

MEJRA   *(suddenly angry)* Pick up the rock.

STETKO   I can't.

> He grins.

Funny thing about "dictators" eh?
What happens when nobody does as they're told?
What's the dictator to do? Kill them all?
Then there'd be nobody left to do all the dirty work.
Then the dictator isn't a dictator anymore.
Maybe everybody is pretending to be who they are.
Maybe everybody has to believe a lie.

MEJRA   And what lie do you want to believe—that I'm here to save
you, or to bury you alive?

STETKO   (*grins*) I believe you like me.
                But you're too old and ugly for a young guy like me.

MEJRA   Too ugly to be raped, too old to be impregnated.
                Just right for killing.

STETKO   For sure. We would have just shot you.

MEJRA   I would have considered myself lucky.

STETKO   Strange world, eh?

MEJRA   What will it be?
                Choose.

                Pause.

                Pick it up.

STETKO   No.

                Pause.

                MEJRA starts digging STETKO's grave with her hands.

                What are you doing?

MEJRA   Guess.

STETKO   You stupid bitch fucking cunt—

                He heaves the rock to his chest.

MEJRA   (*slaps him across the face*) Don't ever call me that again.

STETKO   What's with you?
                I lift it.
                I drop it.
                Doesn't matter what I do I get slapped down.
                You wouldn't touch me if I wasn't tied up.

MEJRA   You wouldn't rape girls if they were armed.

STETKO   (*laughs*) Guess not.
                You think I'm stupid?
                I know they don't like it.

MEJRA   No, they don't.

STETKO	You been raped?
MEJRA	None of your business.
STETKO	I take that for yes.
MEJRA	I don't care how you take it, just understand this, the military is not the only one with power.
STETKO	*(grins)* Untie me, Mejra.
MEJRA	*(grins back)* Not yet, Stinko.
STETKO	This rock is too fucking heavy.
MEJRA	Drop it—except on your foot— and I bury you alive.
STETKO	What is the point of this?
MEJRA	The right to choose.
STETKO	Hold it, break my foot, or be buried alive?!
MEJRA	I knew you had some potential, Stinko.

> *She exits.*

STETKO Don't call me Stinko!
It's Stetko.
Stet-ko Tef-te-dar-i-ja.
Stupid—

> *He stops short just in case she hears him. He holds the rock as the lights indicate the coming of night. He sings a marching tune, baldly, defiantly.*

> *Blackout.*

Djanet Sears (1959–)

HARLEM DUET

1M / 1F

Ten years after *Goodnight Desdemona (Good Morning Juliet)* raised the spotlight on Toronto's Nightwood Theatre, a more tragic reinvention of the Othello story revived this earlier success.

Djanet Sears, like Ann-Marie MacDonald, found Canada's oldest professional feminist theatre to be fertile ground for her creativity. *Harlem Duet*, directed by Sears herself, premiered at Nightwood in 1997 and subsequently won the Chalmers Canadian Play Award, four Dora Awards, and, in 1998, a Governor General's Literary Award. Since then, Djanet Sears has continued to write plays and to be involved in theatre. She began the Obsidian Theatre Company, taught playwriting at the University of Toronto, and has edited the first anthology of plays by Canadians of African descent, titled *Testifyin'* (Playwrights Canada Press, 2000). In 2006, *Harlem Duet* was restaged at the Stratford Festival.

This play is set in the Harlem of the 1990s, using the lover duet of Billie and Othello, a young black couple who have moved to Harlem to live immersed in black culture. Sears's theme of racial identity is set against Shakespeare's themes of jealousy and betrayal. Our playwright achieves more resonance with the use of flashback scenarios between couples set first in 1860, then in 1920, before and after emancipation. To enhance this lyrical synthesis of time, Sears uses a soundscape taken from the speeches of Martin Luther King Jr., Malcolm X, and Jesse Jackson mixed with the music of the blues to transition between scenes. Sears intersperses short scenarios from the earlier settings to recall the history of racism and to engage the tragic refrain of the betrayal of black women by their men. The overall effect of speech, sound, and words is a unity that is hauntingly synaesthetic.

In this scene, Othello has returned to the Harlem apartment he shared with Billie, where he married her by the African-American ceremony of "jumping the broom." His new lover, Mona, is a white woman. Here, what begins as an argument between Billie and Othello over affirmative action (a thinly disguised justification by Othello for his recent betrayal) ends in a hopeful reunion, using words from the lovers' past. Yet the scene that follows has Mona enter Billie's apartment unexpectedly and Othello follows her out dutifully, stunning Billie into amazed silence.

Pause.

OTHELLO I'll be heading the department's courses in Cyprus next summer.

BILLIE I thought you told me Christopher…. What's his name?

OTHELLO Chris Yago?

BILLIE Yeh, Yago.

OTHELLO Well everyone thought he would get it. I thought he'd get it. So a whole bunch of them are challenging affirmative action.

BILLIE Rednecks in academia.

OTHELLO No, no…. Well… I think it's a good thing.

BILLIE Pul-eese.

OTHELLO Using discrimination to cure discrimination is not—

BILLIE We're talking put asides of five percent. Five percent of everything available to whites. They've still got ninety-five.

OTHELLO Billie…. Injustice against blacks can't be cured by injustice against whites… you know that.

BILLIE And younger people won't have the same opportunities you had.

OTHELLO Now look who's sounding white.

BILLIE Who said you sounded white?

OTHELLO It's implied…. No one at school tells me I don't know how to do my job… it's implied. I'll be at a faculty meeting, I'll make a suggestion, and it'll be ignored. Not five minutes later someone else will make the exact same suggestion and everyone will agree to it. Mona noticed it, too. They think I'm only there because I'm black. I've tested it.

BILLIE So let me get this straight, you're against affirmative action in order for white people to respect you.

OTHELLO   For my peers... my peers to respect me. You know what it's like. Every day I have to prove to them that I can do my job. I feel that any error I make only goes to prove them right.

BILLIE   Well you must be perfect. Mona respects you.

OTHELLO   Well, she really sees me. She was the only other faculty to support me on the MLK Day assembly. When we played the video—

BILLIE   The "I have a dream" speech?

OTHELLO   They understood. For a moment I got them to understand.

He picks up several books and places them in a box.

BILLIE   "America has defaulted on this promissory note insofar as her...

OTHELLO & BILLIE
...citizens of colour are concerned.

OTHELLO   Instead of honouring this sacred obligation, America has given its coloured people a...

OTHELLO & BILLIE
bad cheque...

BILLIE   ...a cheque that has come back marked...

OTHELLO & BILLIE
...'insufficient funds.'"

BILLIE   The man was a... a...

OTHELLO   Poet.... Visionary.

BILLIE   A prophet.

OTHELLO   After all he'd been through in his life, he could still see that at a deeper level we're all the same.

Pause.

BILLIE   I'm not the same.

OTHELLO   In the eyes of God, Billie, we're all the same.

BILLIE   One day little black boys and little white girls—

OTHELLO   You're delusional.

BILLIE   You're the one looking for white respect.

OTHELLO   Wrong again! White respect, black respect, it's all the same to me.

BILLIE   Right on, brother man!

OTHELLO   When I was growing up… in a time of black pride—it was something to say you were black. Before that, I'd say…. My family would say we're Cuban…. It takes a long time to work through some of those things. I am a member of the human race.

BILLIE   Oh, that's a switch. What happened to all that J.A. Rogers stuff you were pushing? Blacks created the world, blacks are the progenitors of European civilization, gloriana…. Constantly trying to prove you're as good, no, better than white people. White people are always the line for you, aren't they? The rule… the margin… the variable of control. We are black. Whatever we do is black.

OTHELLO   I'm so tired of this race shit, Billie. There are alternatives—

BILLIE   Like what? Oh yes, white.

OTHELLO   Oh, don't be so—

BILLIE   Isn't that really what not acting black, or feeling black, means.

OTHELLO   Liberation has no colour.

BILLIE   But progress is going to white schools… proving we're as good as whites… like some holy grail… all that we're taught in those white schools. All that is in us. Our success is whiteness. We religiously seek to have what they have. Access to the white-man's world. The white-man's job.

OTHELLO   That's economics.

BILLIE   White economics.

OTHELLO   God! Black women always—

BILLIE   No. Don't even go there…

OTHELLO   I…. You…. Forget it!

BILLIE   *(quietly at first)* Yes, you can forget it, can't you. I don't have
that… that luxury. When I go into a store I always know
when I'm being watched. I can feel it. They want to see if
I'm gonna slip some of their stuff into my pockets. When
someone doesn't serve me I think it's because I'm black. When
a clerk won't put the change into my held-out hand, I think
it's because I'm black. When I hear about a crime, any crime,
I pray to God the person who they think did it isn't black.
I'm even suspicious of the word black. Who called us black
anyway? It's not a country, it's not a racial category, its not
even the colour of my skin. And don't give me this content of
one's character B.S. I'm sorry… I am sorry… I had a dream.
A dream that one day a black man and a black woman might
find…. Where jumping a broom was a solemn eternal vow
that… I…. Let's…. Can we just get this over with?

> *She goes to the window.*
>
> *Silence.*
>
> *He moves toward her.*

OTHELLO   I know… I know. I'm sorry…

BILLIE   Yeh…

OTHELLO   I care… you know that.

BILLIE   I know.

> *Silence.*

OTHELLO   I never thought I'd miss Harlem.

> *Pause.*

BILLIE   You still think it's a reservation?

OTHELLO   Homeland/reservation.

BILLIE   A sea of black faces.

OTHELLO   Africatown, USA.

> *Pause.*

BILLIE	When we lived in the Village, sometimes, I'd be on the subway and I'd miss my stop. And I'd just sit there, past midtown, past the upper west side, and somehow I'd end up here. And I'd just walk. I love seeing all these brown faces.
OTHELLO	Yeh...
BILLIE	Since they knocked down the old projects I can see the Schomberg Museum from here. You still can't make out Harlem Hospital. I love that I can see the Apollo from our— from my balcony.
OTHELLO	Fire escape.
BILLIE	Patio.
OTHELLO	You never did find a pair of lawn chairs and a table to fit in that space.
BILLIE	Terrace.
OTHELLO	I never saw the beauty in it.
BILLIE	Deck. My deck.
OTHELLO	I wish...

He looks at her.

BILLIE	That old building across the street? I didn't know this, but that used to be the Hotel Theresa. That's where Castro stayed when he came to New York.... Must have been the fifties. Ron Brown's father used to run that hotel.
OTHELLO	I... I... I miss you so much sometimes. Nine years... it's a long time.
BILLIE	I know.
OTHELLO	I'm really not trying to hurt you, Billie.
BILLIE	I know.
OTHELLO	I never meant to hurt you.

He strokes her face.

BILLIE	I know.
OTHELLO	God, you're so beautiful.

He kisses her. She does not resist.

BILLIE	I... don't... I feel...

He kisses her again.

What are you doing?

OTHELLO	I... I'm... I'm exploring the heightening Alleghenies of Pennsylvania.

He kisses her again.

The curvaceous slopes of California.

He kisses her again.

The red hills of Georgia, the mighty mountains of New York. Such sad eyes.

He kisses her again.

I'm an equal opportunity employer.

Pause.

I am an equal opportunity employer.

Pause.

I say, I'm an equal opportunity employer, then you say, I don't come...

BILLIE	I don't come cheap, you know.
OTHELLO	I'm offering more than money can buy.
BILLIE	How much more?
OTHELLO	This much.

He kisses her.

BILLIE	I could buy that.
OTHELLO	Could you buy this?

He kisses her deeply.

BILLIE   Be…. Be…. Beloved.

She kisses him.

Kevin Kerr (1968–)

UNITY (1918)

1M / 1F

Kevin Kerr is a graduate of UBC's Department of Theatre and Film and of Vancouver's renowned Studio 58 for theatre professionals. Like many of his contemporaries, he is comfortable as a director or as an actor. Kerr is a founding member and co-artistic director of the Electric Company Theatre of Vancouver, a collective with which he has earned numerous Jessie Richardson Theatre Awards. In 2002, Kevin Kerr won the Governor General's Literary Award as a playwright for *Unity (1918)*.

The end of the Great War brought with it an influenza pandemic that resulted in more deaths of young, Canadian adults than four years of war. Kerr's fictionalized account of this devastation is set ironically in a small Prairie town named Unity, whose citizens are torn apart by the Spanish influenza in the fall of 1918.

Beatrice, age twenty, patriotically knits socks for soldiers overseas and romanticizes about marrying a hero. She is then faced with the reality of Hart, who has returned from war, crippled from the cold, wet trenches and blinded by poison gas only to find no surviving relatives to welcome him back home. His only delight is hearing Bea's voice. Kerr's delicate dialogue threads several touching and often darkly humorous exchanges between these two unlikely lovers, culminating in this scene near the end of the play. Here, Bea tends to Hart who is now, himself, dying of influenza. Bea's final gesture is as uncharacteristic for her as it is fatal; it shows that she, like the others around her who are forced to live in a world without a future, has no choice but to draw her happiness solely from the present.

The mortuary. HART is lying amidst the bodies.
BEATRICE enters.

HART	Sunna?
BEA	No. It's Beatrice. I heard you weren't well.
HART	Where's Sunna?
BEA	In the graveyard.
HART	She's dead?
BEA	No. She's just digging graves.
HART	Who's dead?
BEA	Lots of people.
HART	Me too, soon enough, I guess.
BEA	No. You just have to rest.
HART	What colour are my feet?
BEA	What?
HART	What colour are my feet? I heard a doctor on the train in Montreal say that when the feet turn black there's no hope.

BEATRICE lifts the sheet revealing his feet. They're black.

BEA	Your feet are fine.
HART	I can see the end.
BEA	See the end? Please. You're delirious. You're blind; you can't see the end. Just rest.

She sponges his forehead.

HART	Something has happened.
BEA	What?
HART	I think it's the war.

BEA	Yes, it's over now.
HART	Yes, and something big has happened. A hole.
BEA	What?
HART	I guess it's when there's so much traffic between this world and the next the space between them is stretched out of shape. The wrong people fall over to the other side and angels slip out of heaven and wander around down here bumping into things.
BEA	Hmm?
HART	It's dark down here. Heaven's much brighter and your eyes get used to it. Angels are a clumsy lot if they end up back here. Lots of accidents. Broken things. People pushed by mistake into the other world.
BEA	And are you an angel?
HART	Are you?
BEA	No, I'm just a girl.
HART	The last girl I saw was in France.
BEA	A nurse?
HART	A prostitute.
BEA	Oh.
HART	She was very pretty.
BEA	Oh.
HART	Very pretty.
BEA	Well, I suppose that was good for business.
HART	She was my first.
BEA	Well.
HART	She went to blow out the candles, but I wanted to see.
BEA	Oh?

HART	I said, "Don't blow out the candles." And she said, "*Quoi?*" Just like that. "*Quoi?*" That's funny, huh? "*Quoi?*" I wanted to see her. And then I realized she couldn't see me.
BEA	She couldn't see?
HART	Me. I was invisible to her. But I couldn't do it without being seen. Without her knowing it was me.
BEA	You weren't... ashamed?
HART	Only if I was invisible. I had to do something to make myself be seen. So I placed her hand on my heart and thought really hard, "See this." And her hand on my mouth—again, "See." And the strangest thing was, I began to see myself through her hand. My face, my chest. And then I knew I had never seen myself before.
BEA	But—
HART	No, never. And I wondered if this pretty girl had ever seen herself before. So I placed my hand on her face—"See this." On her neck—"There." Her breasts—"These." Her belly— "Here." And light seemed to flood the room—much more than a candle. And there, her clothes fell away and then I looked down, got down on my knees, and... I guess it was there that I lost my sight.
BEA	There?
HART	There. The last I ever saw.
BEA	You went blind by looking at... her—
	Pause.
	You don't think it was perhaps the gas attack?
HART	No. I don't think so.
BEA	Well, I don't think looking at that can make you blind.
HART	No?
BEA	Well, I'm sure you shouldn't have been looking there, but—
HART	I saw through to the other side.

BEA	Huh?
HART	And the next day we went to battle. And I thought I saw. I thought I saw the guns, the fire, the men falling around me, and the gas, the green-yellow fog... but it was a dream. I had already seen the other side and could see no more. Are you there?
BEA	Yes. Here.

She sponges him some more.

HART	Have you ever seen yourself?
BEA	I... don't know.
HART	Would you like to?
BEA	Yes.
HART	I think that's good.

She watches him breathe for a while. Then slowly she undoes her mask and lets it drop. She softly kisses him on the lips. Very bright light.

Stephen Massicotte (1969–)

MARY'S WEDDING

1M / 1F

Stephen Massicotte has written six prize-winning plays, including *Mary's Wedding*, which itself won four awards: the Alberta Playwriting Competition (2000), the Betty Mitchell Award, and the Gwen Pharis Ringwood Award for Drama (2003). His remarkable range as a writer is a strength and is characteristic of his generation of Canadian playwrights. In addition to *Mary's Wedding*, Massicotte has written successful cult horror films *(Ginger Snaps Back)*, television scripts for Disney *(Honey, I Shrunk the Kids)*, comedy for CBC *(Tom Stone)*, and black comedy for the stage *(Spot the Pervert)*. Massicotte's most recent accolade (the Carol Bolt Award, 2007) is for the drama *The Oxford Roof Climber's Rebellion* (2006). It juxtaposes the post-war trauma of two of the twentieth century's most famous men, Robert Graves and T.E. Lawrence (known more famously as Lawrence of Arabia) when they meet at the world's most famous university in 1920.

Massicotte's fascination with World War I is not unique. The tearing apart of families and rending of entire communities between 1914 and 1918 have compelled Canadian writers of fiction, poetry, and drama to express this crucial era like no other. It is now almost historical cliché to say that out of Canada's enormous contribution to World War I a nation was born—and so was a vast segment of our national literature.

Mary's Wedding is set in 1914. The power of this piece is as a universal love story told in a unique way to reveal both the romance of war and its brutal consequences; in the playwright's words, the "poetry" of war and its "real life." Massicotte gives his audience just enough dialogue to conjure for us a compelling and beautiful young romance between Mary and Charlie. Yet, just as we expect the heroic soldier to return from battle to Mary's waiting arms, the playwright rips him away forever.

Massicotte sets his play in Mary's dream the night before her marriage to another man. His creative use of the dream sequence, especially in this, the last scene of the play, lends a brilliant poignancy. Ironically, in Mary's dream it is she who must tell Charlie how he has died in battle. Mary must also deal with her guilt; earlier she had not seen him off to war knowing she couldn't handle the pain of the marriage proposal she knew he was going to make the night before his departure.

CHARLIE waits for MARY in the barn.

MARY   And this is how it ends. I never went to see him, but in this dream I do. We're in the barn. Charlie is. He is waiting for me. Nervous and shy, waiting to sail away on the grey ship full of horses.

He waited the night that I never came to say goodbye. It's the night he waited to ask me and he left the next morning. But in this dream I go to see him. I go to stop him. I go to tell him.

CHARLIE   Mary?

I'm glad you came.

MARY   You didn't think I would, did you?

CHARLIE   I wasn't too sure.

MARY   So, you're going?

CHARLIE   I am. I am. I have to. It'll be over soon. We'll take them in a charge outside of a year. That's what they're all saying. We'll be home by Christmas. It won't seem that long and I'll be home.

CHARLIE is less convinced of this than he was.

I'll write you non-stop, you'll see. Your mailbox will be full all the time. I promise. You won't even miss me.

MARY   Yes, I will. Yes, I do. I miss you very badly. Every minute.

CHARLIE   It'll be over before you...

MARY   Charlie...

CHARLIE   Then we can be married.

MARY   Yes, that would be wonderful.

CHARLIE   It'll be sunny. You'll be in one of those pretty white dresses and we can have our portrait taken and we can have children. We'll have children, not right away. Two girls and one boy...

MARY   Two boys and one girl.

CHARLIE	...and we'll have horses for all the little colonists.
MARY	Charlie, listen, for a minute, please. It sounds lovely but... just listen. I went to get the post today.
CHARLIE	Did I write?
MARY	There wasn't anything there.
CHARLIE	Oh. Well, I bet there will be something tomorrow. Or the day after. You know how slow the mail is.
MARY	There won't be any more letters.
CHARLIE	Sure, there will. I write you all the time. I just promised.
MARY	The last one that arrived was the one after the charge at Moreuil Wood. The one where you told me you wanted to come home. You said, "I want to come home now. I want to meet you in our barn. I never want to leave you again."

Something is slowly dawning on CHARLIE.

CHARLIE	What is it, Mary? What happened?
MARY	I met your father today in town.
CHARLIE	How's he doing? I miss him already.
MARY	He misses you, too. The farm is well. There are two new mares. He said that he'd... that he'd gotten a message. News.
CHARLIE	Did Flowers get his medal?
MARY	Yes.
CHARLIE	Lieutenant Gordon Muriel Flowerdew, Victoria Cross.
MARY	It's hard to forget a name like that. No, it was a telegram. You and the Canadian Cavalry Division stopped the German advance. Some say you saved the war.
CHARLIE	That's good, isn't it?
MARY	It is good, I suppose. I'm trying. I'm trying. You were in a field. You and all of your tents. A German plane flew by at night and strafed the regiment while you were camped.
CHARLIE	Was anyone hurt?

> *She shakes her head.*

MARY　　*(whispers)* No.

CHARLIE　　How about the horses?

MARY　　No, but they were scattered… and you had to… all of you had to go and find them where they'd run off to. And it took all night to find the horses and… the German artillery was shelling places where there might be regiments camped out. They just dropped three or four every now and then, in case they might get… in case they might happen to drop some shells on someone who might happen to be out there. Out there looking for their horses.

CHARLIE　　They do that all the time. It's a sign that we've got them on the run, that they're getting desperate. The fight is out of them.

MARY　　But Charlie, I have to tell you… I have to tell you. You've come and found her in a field. She wakes up from her dream and stands up. You touch her and step by her neck and shoulder. You calm her. The sun is rising. You're happy. She's happy. She is unhurt and you can bring her back home. I dream it all the time.

CHARLIE　　That's when they shelled the field?

MARY　　I swear you hear them. You look up at the sky. The two of you don't move and I always wonder why. You just stand beside her looking up at the sky.

CHARLIE　　We're going to count the thousands from the flash to the rumble.

MARY　　Yes.

CHARLIE　　Before they land… before I… before I die… do I say anything?

MARY　　Yes. Something. I can't make it out. I'm sorry.

CHARLIE　　I guess we won't be getting married. I guess we don't.

MARY　　I'm sorry.

CHARLIE　　I'm sorry, too.

> *MARY holds CHARLIE's face in her hands.*

MARY	I nearly die of heartache. I swear, for months I can't move. For months I float down the river with my name on the prow.
CHARLIE	But you get better though.
MARY	I do.
CHARLIE	You don't die.
MARY	I live.
CHARLIE	You love someone good. Please tell me you marry someone good?
MARY	Not yet. Tomorrow.
CHARLIE	Just love him as well as you can and be happy. Please.
MARY	I'm sorry, Charlie, I'm sorry I never came to see you in the barn.
CHARLIE	You did tonight.
MARY	I'm sorry I never stopped you from going.
CHARLIE	You did tonight.
MARY	I'm so sorry. It's the worst thing I ever did. And I can't forget you.
CHARLIE	Don't forget. Just let go.
MARY	I'm trying to. It's just you're in everything. All the time.
CHARLIE	Let me be in everything. Just a little less maybe.
MARY	Will you always be there?
CHARLIE	Yes, Mary, always. Only a little less. I've got to go now.
	A far-off roll of thunder sounds. MARY and CHARLIE look to it.
MARY	No, don't go. Don't go. Please, stay with me.
CHARLIE	I can't stay. I have to go now and it's time for you to wake up.
MARY	I can't.
CHARLIE	Yes, you can.

MARY	Please, don't go. Kiss me, please.

They kiss. They hold on very tight.

CHARLIE	I love you.
MARY	I love you so much.
CHARLIE	You… you are the best thing, the very best thing. I'll see you someday.
MARY	I hope so. I do hope so.

CHARLIE slowly lets go of MARY.

There's a thunderstorm coming.

CHARLIE	I don't mind getting a little wet.
MARY	What are you going to do?
CHARLIE	I don't know. I think… I think I'll just go and… I think I'll just go for a ride… I'll just go out for a little ride in the fields. Just enjoy the rain for a little while.

MARY's composure begins to slip.

Don't worry, it'll be over by the time you wake up. Mary's wedding will be sunny. You'll never dream this again. In a little while you are going to wake up and I will have been lying under the grass for nearly two years now. You are going to wake up and you will never have this dream again. And when you wake up this is what I see:

I see you in a white dress at the church. I see your mother and friends helping you with your hair and yellow flowers. And you are beautiful. I can see tears on your face as you walk down the aisle with all your friends and family smiling for you. People think you are crying because of all the excitement. You walk slowly with your face looking at the floor. You try very hard to take every step. And just before you get up to the front, your eyes slowly rise and you see the face of the good man you are going to marry. And slowly, like a sunrise, you smile and your heart is like the clear blue sky. You smile, Mary.

And outside a soft wind blows, and in that wind there is the very faint sound of a horse riding in the fields.

Just barely it's there, faint in the summer wind.

MARY   How do you know?

CHARLIE Because I'm in it.

The sound of a light breeze can be heard. CHARLIE stands off in the deep blue, but is not gone.

MARY   And that's the end of the dream. It begins at the end and ends at the beginning. Like before, Charlie rides away thinking of me, only this time he doesn't go away. This time there is no more war. This time he rides off into the fields.

When I awake, the day, my dress, and my husband are waiting. It's a July wedding on a Saturday morning in nineteen hundred and twenty. I still think of him.

I see him on horses. I see him running with them, in dreams, in waking, in forests, in evenings, and in mornings. I hear him laughing and riding swiftly through fields. I hear him in church bells. I see white dresses, flowers, and little babies, and Charlie is there in all of it. Only, now a little less. Only, now a little bit less. And that will be enough. Goodbye, Charlie.

CHARLIE Goodbye, Mary. Do you want to know what I say before the shells land?

MARY   Yes, please.

CHARLIE Wake up, Mary, wake up.

They smile at each other from a distance. Then, as they leave separately, the wind rises a little and the church bells ring. Behind that, farther off as the sun rises, a single horse rides away into the distance.

All of this is very pretty.

TEMPTING PROVIDENCE

1M / 1F

Robert Chafe is a Newfoundland playwright who was commissioned in 2000 to write a biographical play about Nurse Myra Bennett. Bennett left Britain in 1921 for a two-year stint in the colony as the only medical professional for three hundred miles of Newfoundland coastline. She spent the next seventy years there, devoting her life to the people of Newfoundland's rugged shore.

Initially, *Tempting Providence* was planned by director Jillian Keiley of Theatre Newfoundland and Labrador as a straightforward production with the intention of playing nursing homes in the province. Since then, it has played to over twenty-eight thousand people in two hundred twenty-eight performances in sixty-four cities over three continents. It placed Robert Chafe on the Governor General's short list for 2004 and contributed to Jillian Keiley receiving the one hundred thousand dollar Elinore and Lou Siminovitch Prize, Canada's richest theatre award.

Chafe's plays have been described by the Governor General's Award jury as having characters that "vibrate with fight and humanity, [and] dialogue [that] sparkles with tension and surprise." In this brief interlude, Nurse Myra has caught the eye of her future husband, Angus Bennett, as they both take a break from a traditional Newfoundland kitchen party. It is a simple scene, but reveals a depth of character and feeling that "would make the very Atlantic blush with shame," to steal the beautiful personification Angus himself uses to charm Myra.

MYRA and ANGUS step out on the porch.

MYRA   My lord, it is hot in there.

ANGUS   Is that why we are out here?

MYRA   You people, it's amazing. This perfectly nice house, with a perfectly nice parlour, couches, chairs, and you all insist upon squeezing into a kitchen the size of a closet.

ANGUS   It's a proper dance, my dear. Can't stray from the kitchen.

MYRA   Really.

ANGUS   You complaining?

MYRA   What?

ANGUS   You weren't having fun?

MYRA   I simply said it was hot.

ANGUS   Think I didn't notice the circle you were spinning around that room with Alex? Cut a path right into the floorboards, no doubt. I told Mother not to invite you, you would only do damage.

MYRA   I didn't say I wasn't enjoying myself, Mr. Bennett.

ANGUS   You're just hot.

MYRA   Warm. Yes. Too warm.

ANGUS   Now see, that sounds like the words of a woman who is not planning on walking back into that kitchen for one more dance.

MYRA   I honestly don't think I'm up for it.

ANGUS   You are going home after having the last dance with Alex. That's not a slap in the face, is it?

MYRA   Your brother was very insistent.

ANGUS   Runs in the family. Just like our dancing. Give me half the chance, I'll prove it.

MYRA   Your insistence?

ANGUS   You're not going home yet.

MYRA   Excuse me?

ANGUS   Unless you want half the town thinking you're only after younger men.

MYRA   Inappropriate, Mr. Bennett.

ANGUS   I agree. Doesn't become you.

MYRA   Stop it. What do I have to say? What would you have me do?

ANGUS   Take five minutes. Long enough to catch your breath.

>   *Another silent standoff. She holds his gaze and then looks up at the sky.*

MYRA   Lovely night. You have a lot of them here.

ANGUS   Yes. I keep forgetting that our beloved nurse has only been with us since the spring. She has not had the pure pleasure of a Newfoundland winter.

MYRA   You all have this big talk about winter. Like it's a terror. You're not frightening me. I don't scare off that easily.

ANGUS   No?

MYRA   I, my dear man, have battled and braved worse foes than your much vilified Newfoundland winter.

ANGUS   So you think.

MYRA   You are so smug, Mr. Bennett. How can you be sure that I do not have a fondness for a little snow and wind?

>   *He laughs.*

            How can you be sure, Mr. Bennett, that your lengthy winter is not one of the reasons I chose to come to Newfoundland in the first place?

ANGUS   Was it?

MYRA	As a matter of fact, yes.
ANGUS	Our winters and our kitchen parties.

A small pause.

What were your reasons?

MYRA	What?
ANGUS	Why did you come here?

A small pause.

MYRA	No great secret, I wanted to help. I wanted to help people.
ANGUS	Newfoundlanders.
MYRA	Newfoundlanders. Anybody.
ANGUS	Could of helped anybody in England. Didn't need to come all the way over here to do that.
MYRA	It was a question of need. There was a great and saddening need here. I read a story about a family in Saskatchewan. I originally applied to go there, and was told I was needed more here.
ANGUS	One story about one family and you packed up your life?
MYRA	A young mother, her first child. Her and her husband lived quite a distance out. Quite a few days travel to anybody else. He left to get help. Left as soon as they thought the baby might be on its way. Weather set in. Help was too far away. Hours turn into days. Story has a sad ending.
ANGUS	And that was that? Duty calls?
MYRA	Stories about mothers and babies deserve only the happiest of endings.

A small pause. He smiles at her.

ANGUS	They are all afraid of you, you know. Terrified. Gotta do what the nurse says or else.

She looks at the sky silently.

It's just the way you talk to them.

MYRA	It's necessary sometimes, to make myself clear, and listened to.
ANGUS	Oh, you don't have to tell me. It's just... I think they see this one side of you. They see this nurse. A very good nurse, well-respected, don't get me wrong. But they just see that side. And, that's a shame. Because... I get the feeling that Nurse Grimsley has a depth that would make the very Atlantic blush with shame.

She remains staring at the sky.

MYRA	Mr. Bennett—
ANGUS	Your five minutes are up.

She looks at him.

Do you have your breath?

A warm pause.

MYRA	I believe so.
ANGUS	Yes?
MYRA	Take me back to your hot and crowded kitchen. If you must.

ANGUS laughs.

ANGUS	If I must?
MYRA	If you must, take me to your kitchen, sir. Dance me until my legs themselves plead for clemency.

Fast dancing and music. ANGUS breaks away.

ANGUS	She stayed for two more hours that night. Only danced with me twice. Danced with every other guy there. With Alex four or five times. Didn't matter though. She could have danced with anyone she pleased. She could have refused me a dance outright. For she smiled at few of them. She talked to even less. And with me, with me she took her five-minute breaks, which stretched to twenty. Empty porch step. Cold colouring our breath. Long talks circling nothing. Stars the only witnesses.

ANGUS joins up with her again. Dancing and music.

PART TWO

Scenes for Three

Daniel MacIvor (1962–)

NEVER SWIM ALONE

2M / 1F

Daniel MacIvor is an actor, playwright, and director from Sydney, Nova Scotia, who was educated at Dalhousie University and George Brown College. MacIvor is most closely associated with the Toronto theatre company he founded, da da kamera, serving as artistic director from 1986 to 2007, and it is in this creative flourish of his early career in theatre that *Never Swim Alone* was born.

This three-character, one-act play is characteristic of MacIvor's playwriting, as is the postmodern style that treats the audience as theatre participant and mixes monologue with dialogue in a creative free-for-all reminiscent of the alienation techniques of agitprop. In *Never Swim Alone*, two similarly dressed businessmen are run through a series of verbal competitions, or "rounds," essentially power and status games that recall their lives past and present. Each round is judged by a mysterious girl in a bathing suit who sits upstage centre in a lifeguard chair and acts as a referee, awarding points and noting fouls. Eventually, the audience learns the mystery: she drowned as a result of the competitive swim "to the point" she initiates when all three are adolescents.

MacIvor shines a unique light in Canadian theatre. His plays have won a Chalmers, two Doras, and the Governor General's Literary Award in 2006 for *I Still Love You*, a collection of five of his plays. He has also received five award nominations for his screenplays, including two Genies, and won the Atlantic Canada Award for best actor (2005) for the film, *Whole New Thing*, for which he also wrote the screenplay.

FRANK & BILL
    No one is perfect.

BILL   By William (Bill) Wade

FRANK   and A. Francis DeLorenzo. No one is perfect.

BILL   No one. Were our fathers perfect? Certainly not.

FRANK   Were our mothers perfect?

FRANK & BILL
    Perhaps.

BILL   But I am not my mother.

FRANK & BILL
    No.

FRANK   Nor is my wife my mother.

BILL   No.

FRANK   Nor will she ever be, as much as I might wish she were, as hard as she might try.

BILL   Frank?

FRANK   I digress.
    Am I perfect?

BILL   Am I perfect?

FRANK & BILL
    No.

FRANK   Yet, let us consider a moment—

BILL   —a moment—

FRANK   —that I am not myself—

BILL   —myself—

FRANK   —but rather—

FRANK & BILL
—someone else.

FRANK   Then as this person—

BILL   —I could—

FRANK   —watch me—

BILL   —take note—

FRANK   —take note—

FRANK & BILL
—of all the things I do—

BILL   —the small selfishness—

FRANK   —the minor idiosyncrasies—

FRANK & BILL
—the tiny spaces—

BILL   —between me—

FRANK & BILL
—and perfection.

FRANK   Perhaps then it would—

FRANK & BILL
—be e... be e... be easier—

BILL   —to see—

FRANK   —to look at me—

BILL   —and see—

FRANK & BILL
—be e... be e... be easier—

FRANK   —to change.

FRANK & BILL
But of course, if I was someone else I would have my own
problems to deal with.

FRANK   So what is perfect?

BILL   What?

FRANK   Besides tomorrow.

FRANK & BILL
             Ah, tomorrow!

BILL   Because tomorrow is an endless possibility—

FRANK & BILL
             —and an endless possibility is the second best thing to wake
             up next to.

FRANK   But what? Let us consider a moment...

BILL   ...a note.

FRANK & BILL
             A note.

BILL	**FRANK**
Laaaaaaaaaaaaaaaaaaaaaaaa aaaaaaaaaaaaaaaaaaaaaaaaa aaaaaaaaaaaaaaaaaaaaaaaaa aaaaaaaaaaaaaaaaaaaaaaaaa aaaaaaaaaaaaaaaaaaaaaaaaa aaa.	At first faltering and self-conscious then building up then pushed forward then gaining commitment then losing breath and trailing off near the end.

BILL   But in it there was something—

FRANK & BILL
             —perfect.

FRANK   A happy accident?

BILL   A fluke?

FRANK   Mere chance?

FRANK & BILL
             Perhaps. But back to me.

FRANK   And me—

BILL   —for all my weakness—

FRANK   —as a note—

FRANK & BILL
             —let's say—

BILL   —a note stretched out from birth—

FRANK & BILL
              —to death,

FRANK   I will allow—

BILL   —that here and there—

FRANK   —from time to time—

BILL   —there is a sound—

FRANK   —a thought—

BILL   —a word—

FRANK & BILL
              —that touches on perfection.

BILL   But overall—

FRANK   —and wholly, no—

FRANK & BILL
              —I know—

FRANK   —I am not perfect.

FRANK & BILL
              I know—

BILL   —I am not perfect.

FRANK & BILL
              But as not perfect as I am, he's a whole hell of a lot more not
              perfect than me.

              FRANK and BILL resume their seats.

REFEREE   Halftime.

              REFEREE comes down centre.

              This is the beach. Here is the bay. There is the point.

              FRANK and BILL come down and join her on either side.

REFEREE		FRANK & BILL

REFEREE	This is the beach. Here is the bay. There is the point. This is the beach. Here is the bay. There is the point. This is the beach. Here is the bay. There is the point. Race you to the point? Sun. Boys. Sand. Water. Summer.	**FRANK & BILL** On the beach. At the bay. On the beach. At the bay. On the beach. At the bay. On the beach at the bay. On the beach at the bay. On the beach at the bay.

FRANK   On the beach at the bay.

BILL   Every day that summer.

FRANK   On the beach at the bay.

BILL   All day, every day.

FRANK   On the beach at the bay.

BILL   Every day that summer.

FRANK   On the beach at the bay.

BILL   All summer long.

REFEREE   It is the last day of summer before school begins. Two boys and the girl. She lies in the sun in her blue bathing suit on her green beach towel with her yellow radio. And I could tell you little things about her. I could tell you that her name was Lisa. I could tell you that she had a big brother. I could tell you that she loved horses and lilacs and going to the movies. But that doesn't matter now, all that matters is she is here on the beach with the two boys. The boys watch the girl. She stares out past the point to where the sea makes a line on the sky. The boys are silent and shy. She can hear them blush. She reminds one boy of his sister, she reminds the other of a picture of a woman he once saw in a magazine. The boys simply watch the girl.

FRANK and BILL sing a verse of a summer song.

The sun hangs about there, just over the point. She is a little
drowsy. She gets up and wanders to the edge of the water. She
looks out. She feels a breeze. She turns her head a little over her
shoulder and speaks to the boys:

"Race you to the point?"

> *Through the following the girl walks to the edge of the stage,
> they slowly assume racing positions.*

This is the beach.
Here is the bay.
There is the point.
This is the beach.
Here is the bay.
There is the point.
There is…

FRANK & BILL
  On the beach.
  At the bay.

REFEREE   There is…

FRANK & BILL
  On the beach at the bay.

REFEREE   There is…

FRANK & BILL
  On the beach at the bay.

REFEREE   There is…

FRANK & BILL
  On the beach at the bay.

REFEREE   There is the point.

FRANK   And we sat—

BILL   —on the sand—

FRANK   —at the edge—

BILL	—of the point—
FRANK	—and we waited—
BILL	—and waited…
REFEREE	Race you to the point? Do you remember?
FRANK	One.
BILL	Two.
REFEREE	I remember, too.

I remember. Three!

> *REFEREE resumes her position on chair. She blows her whistle to end halftime. FRANK and BILL return to their chairs.*

Recap: Two men enter a room. A taller man and a shorter man. And each man carries a briefcase. The first man seems very much like the second man and the second man seems very much like the first man, but they are not.

FRANK & BILL	No.
REFEREE	They are not for two reasons. One: one man is the first man and two: one man in his briefcase has a gun.
BILL	A gun.
FRANK	A gun.
REFEREE	Which man is the first man and which man has the gun?

Round Seven: "Dad."

> *REFEREE begins the round. FRANK and BILL approach one another at centre. FRANK does the "what's-on-your-tie" gag to BILL, ending in a nose flick. BILL shoves FRANK. FRANK shoves BILL. BILL shoves FRANK, knocking him down. REFEREE calls a foul on BILL. FRANK and BILL circle one another.*

FRANK	How's your dad?

BILL	Why?
FRANK	I always liked your dad.
BILL	Really?
FRANK	Yeah.
BILL	Well. I always liked your dad.
FRANK	Really?
BILL	Yeah.

FRANK & BILL
    Gee.

FRANK	Your dad was a real easygoing guy.
BILL	Your dad was a real card.
FRANK	Your dad was a real dreamer.
BILL	Your dad was a real character.
FRANK	Your dad was a real nice guy.
BILL	He was a real maniac.
FRANK	He was a real boozer.
BILL	Ha. He was a real wild man.
FRANK	A real cuckold.
BILL	A real wiener.
FRANK	A real dick.
BILL	A real prick.
FRANK	A lemming.
BILL	A fascist.
FRANK	An ass.
BILL	A pig! How's your mom?

        REFEREE ends the round. She calls a tie.

FRANK and BILL speak simultaneously, the capitalized
phrases timed out to be spoken in unison.

FRANK	**BILL**
Please be warned that if you think I'm going to stand here and start dishing dirt and airing laundry about HIS FATHER.	Now this is more than name calling here, although of course that is the temptation, but HIS FATHER
I won't.	drove his mother crazy.
But let's just say the desperation he displays comes from HIS FATHER.	I mean she did have a drinking problem but HIS FATHER
Not that I'm sure he wasn't a well-intentioned, ill-educated man but, an education isn't everything, but	didn't help at all. She spent the last fifteen years in and out of detox as a result of his antics.
FOR EXAMPLE: Rather than face the criminal charges HIS FATHER	FOR EXAMPLE: At the Girl Guide Boy Scout banquet in grade eight HIS FATHER
implied he could not multiply eight times nine when HIS FATHER	was supposed to make a presentation, but when the time came HIS FATHER
's company was missing some seventy-two thousand dollars at the year-end audit. HIS FATHER	was nowhere to be found. Twenty minutes later five guys from the sixth pack found HIS FATHER
claimed he had marked down twenty-four. Twenty-four? Give me a break. AND THAT'S JUST ONE EXAMPLE.	in the boiler room with Suzie Walsh, a sixteen-year-old Girl Guide. AND THAT'S JUST ONE EXAMPLE.
Dishonest?	Is he like that?
Well he did admit to an ignorance in arithmetic and— WELL I'M SURE YOU KNOW WHAT THEY SAY ABOUT FATHERS AND SONS	Well they say a guy and his father are— WELL I'M SURE YOU KNOW WHAT THEY SAY ABOUT FATHERS AND SONS

FRANK	**BILL**
—and far be it, far be it indeed for me to say that	—and I'm not saying they're right all the time, but in this case
HE IS THE PERFECT EXAMPLE. THANK YOU.	HE IS THE PERFECT EXAMPLE. THANK YOU.

REFEREE Pardon me?

FRANK and BILL repeat the above at twice the speed.

Thank you.

FRANK & BILL
You're welcome.

THREE IN THE BACK, TWO IN THE HEAD

2M / 1F

After studying at York University, Jason Sherman began his playwriting career in 1991 with *A League of Nathans*. It was an impressive start, garnering both a Dora nomination and a Chalmers Award. The same two distinctions followed the production of *Three in the Back, Two in the Head* in 1994, in addition to the GG for best play in English in 1995. Sherman has also edited play anthologies and a literary magazine and worked as playwright-in-residence at both Tarragon and Necessary Angel theatres in Toronto.

Three in the Back, Two in the Head is a dark play about a rogue Canadian scientist during the Cold War who is murdered by the CIA. Disillusioned by a US double-cross, Donald Jackson sells the plans to "Snowman," his missile defence system, to a foreign power known only as SI, who use it to attack without fear a neighbouring power, AD. The plot follows an attempt by his son, Paul, an assistant professor unfamiliar with the murky, military world in which his father moved, to uncover the mystery surrounding his father's death, detailed so grimly by the play's title.

Sherman employs an effective flashback technique to reveal pieces of the jigsaw Paul uncovers in the story of his father's secret and tragic life. The playwright uses italics for characters who "speak outside of the scene;" that is, commenting, chorus-like, on the action that typically proceeds in flashback during most of the play. The result is often a stichomythia that strikes an effective rhythm, particularly in this scene. Anna, Paul's mother, observes her son grilling a CIA agent, Doyle, who gradually reveals details about Donald Jackson's murder.

DOYLE's office. DOYLE and PAUL.

DOYLE   You let him go.

PAUL   He said he wanted to go.

DOYLE   And you—knowing as you did that—knowing—

PAUL   You weren't there.

DOYLE   He was your father, and you couldn't tell—

PAUL   He said he wanted to come back to us, to come back—

DOYLE   To "nothing"?

ANNA   *Pauly...*

DOYLE   ...I have, in my file... the report...

ANNA   *Something I didn't tell you...*

DOYLE   ...the report which the gentleman from AD sent following the culmination of the program...

ANNA   *...after your father met with John Doyle...*

DOYLE   ...There were two agents waiting at the graveyard...

ANNA   *...when your father came to me...*

DOYLE   ...when you and your mother arrived...

ANNA   *...in the hotel room...*

DOYLE   They observed him "crawling among the graves"...

ANNA   *...on his hands and knees...*

DOYLE   When your father left you...

ANNA   *...crawling...*

DOYLE   the agents followed him.

ANNA   *...crying...*

DOYLE   They followed him into a church.

ANNA	*…and when I saw him like that…*
DOYLE	They made no attempt to hide themselves from view.
ANNA	*…there was a part of me…*
DOYLE	Your father entered the confession box.
ANNA	*…a part of me I didn't know I had…*
DOYLE	He left the confessional and "walked to where we sat"—
ANNA	*…a part of me that was glad…*
DOYLE	I am quoting directly from the—
ANNA	*…glad to see him on his hands and knees…*
DOYLE	"He attempted to make eye contact."
ANNA	*…a part of me that was thinking:*
DOYLE	"He turned his back to us and knelt."
ANNA	*…forgive me for this…*
DOYLE	The agents stood and fired.
ANNA	*…it's finished…*
DOYLE	The first bullet went through his skull…
ANNA	*…it's over…*
DOYLE	…entered his brain, exited through his forehead. Would you like me to continue…?
ANNA	*…it's over…*
DOYLE	The force of the first bullet knocked your father to the floor.
ANNA	*…the man you were is dead…*
DOYLE	He lay there, probably dead already.
ANNA	*…the man I loved will come back to me…*
DOYLE	The agents stepped forward and fired again.
ANNA	*…I might get you back now…*
DOYLE	The second shot went into his back.

ANNA	*...I won't be alone...*
DOYLE	Two more shots were fired into his spine...
ANNA	*...you won't leave me alone...*
DOYLE	...a fifth into the head...
ANNA	*...you've left me alone...*
DOYLE	...up close, to be sure.
ANNA	*They took this man from me, Pauly. Find out who did this. Bring me their names. Their faces. Their blood for his blood. Their names for his. Bring me something.*
DOYLE	We have all lost something, Paul. You came to me seeking justice. I open my file to you, and I say, "justice has been done." Do you see what I'm saying?
PAUL	Yes. I mean, I understand what you are "saying." You are saying you ordered my father's termination.
DOYLE	Not at all.
PAUL	No, you are saying, "the men from AD" killed my father.
DOYLE	Well, I am saying your father—
PAUL	I don't believe you.
DOYLE	Well that is...
PAUL	I'll take these men.
DOYLE	"Take"?
PAUL	You say the men from AD. Say it again, not in here, not "between you and me," but in public, out there, where I need them, an inquiry, a senate investigation, as a first step to restoring his—
DOYLE	That's—
PAUL	His name.
DOYLE	That's imposs—
PAUL	I want—

DOYLE   That's impossible.

PAUL   I want—names.

DOYLE   "Names."

PAUL   The names of the men who killed my father.

DOYLE   I can't give—

PAUL   Goddamn you, you can give me whatever it is I need.
         I need this.

DOYLE   Paul, it isn't—

PAUL   You *will* give me their names. He gave me the one thing, the
         only thing he knew I could use to protect him.

                    PAUL hands DOYLE some papers.

DOYLE   What is this?

PAUL   This is Snowman, some of Snowman, photocopies of, of the
         codes, figures, I blacked out—but there is enough for you, or
         someone, to verify the, and I am willing, I will give you—in,
         exchange—

DOYLE   "In exchange"—?

PAUL   In exchange for *his* name, *their* names.

DOYLE   For *this*?

PAUL   My father believed in *this*, died for *this*. And I went to Ed
         Sparrow. I said I had Snowman and he told me to come to you,
         because you are the one who has to come forward, because you
         are an "honourable" man, and you will allow the truth to be
         told. He said you would help me.

DOYLE   Ed Sparrow said this.

PAUL   And, in exchange for your help, he would take Snowman.

DOYLE   Ed Sparrow would.

PAUL   Yes. Yes. And he knows, and I will tell you, so that you know,
         that I will destroy Snowman if I am not given what I want.

DOYLE   And you think it's that simple.

PAUL   Yes, I do, think it's that simple, for you to send another cable. I do think that you can make something happen.

DOYLE   I'll have to… because this means nothing to me. Will you wait?

Allan Stratton (1951–)

THE PHOENIX LOTTERY

2M / 1F

Canada's most-accomplished playwright of well-paced, entertaining comedy, Stratton's professional writing career began in the early 1980s with the much-produced farce *Nurse Jane Goes To Hawaii*. Since then, his works have earned a Dora Mavor Moore, a Chalmers, and the Canadian Authors Association's Carol Bolt Award. *The Phoenix Lottery* highlights this playwright's skills as a satirist—from short darts to broadsword gashes that lay bare the pretense of corporation, state, religion, and the arts. Stratton is Neil Simon with a social conscience.

The playwright builds his comedy around Junior Beamish whose father, Edgar, returns from the dead to belittle Junior's socialist plans for the company he built, as he says, on the sound principles of capitalism. Think Hamlet meets the Bronfman family; distill with plenty of visual and verbal comedy, and you have *The Phoenix Lottery*.

In the first scene, the audience learns that Junior has run Edgar's brewery empire into near bankruptcy. In order to raise the firm from the ashes and to support his socialist ambitions, Junior plans to raise a half billion dollars through the globally televised "Phoenix Lottery"—the public torching his father's proudest possession, the priceless "Self-Portrait" by Vincent Van Gogh.

In this scene (from the second act), Emily, the company's executive secretary, desperately wishes for one last supernatural encounter with Edgar, her old boss and secret lover. To up the ante, Emily is also revealed to be Junior's real mother, unbeknownst to him. Unfortunately, Emily cannot hear the ghostly Edgar's pleas, nor feel his loving embrace. Wichita, a papal emissary sent to salvage the Van Gogh, is, of course, the only character (other than Junior) with the ability to communicate with him. Only, His Eminence is not in the mood for ghostly chit-chat. In this scene, Stratton masterfully exploits the classic devices of farce and dramatic irony.

EMILY   Edgar? Are you there? Edgar? If you're there please give me a sign? I want to see you. I need to see you. Please? You're still angry with me, aren't you? Why did you have to die angry with me? Why? You didn't let me explain. You didn't give me a chance to say I was sorry. You just died. You just died and I came in to work the next day with a new silk tie, the kind you liked, all gift-wrapped with a card to say I was sorry, I didn't mean it, only they said you weren't coming in and you'd never be coming in again and I wouldn't be able to see you anymore. And I wouldn't be able to say I was sorry. And I hate you for leaving me like that. Dear God, Edgar, my last memory of you is of you sitting there with that hurt look in your eyes and me slamming the door. It isn't fair, dammit. It isn't fair. I loved you.

            BEAMISH appears.

BEAMISH   Emily?

            EMILY is never able to hear BEAMISH.

EMILY   You used to tease me. You called me a Baptist prude.

BEAMISH   I didn't mean any harm.

EMILY   Well maybe I don't wear dresses that leave nothing to the imagination. But I don't know many Baptist prudes who check into the Park Plaza with a married man. For twenty years, I lived in terror I'd bump into somebody from church or the bridge club. I'd go up the elevators and walk through the halls pretending to read the *Globe and Mail.*

BEAMISH   Two inches in front of your nose.

EMILY   You thought it was funny.

BEAMISH   It was.

EMILY   But I didn't think it was funny. It went against everything I believed. But inside those rooms…. Those were the happiest days of my life.

BEAMISH   And mine.

EMILY   Of course, you were always in a hurry. The first time, I thought the cabby must be outside with the meter running. Heavens to Betsy, I barely had time to turn out the lights before you let out a holler, rolled over, and snored.

BEAMISH   Pardon?

EMILY   I didn't think it had happened. Except it hurt. I was convinced sex was like amnesia with a dentist.

BEAMISH   You're saying I was a bad lover?

EMILY   It was two years before I figured out what all the fuss was about.

BEAMISH   Why didn't you tell me?

EMILY   There was always so much you didn't want to know: How I was feeling. What I was thinking.

BEAMISH   That's not true.

EMILY   You'd say, "Is that all?" and turn on the TV.

BEAMISH   I did?

EMILY   I'll never forget the day I put my foot down. "I'm a Baptist, dammit. You make me feel like a two-bit whore. It's her or me." And when you said you weren't going to divorce her, it tore me apart.

BEAMISH   I couldn't hurt her like that.

EMILY   "You always hurt the ones you love."
            Shakespeare has nothing on the Mills Brothers.

BEAMISH   Please, try to understand.

EMILY   I'll never understand. After everything you said. After everything you promised. I stormed out of this office with you looking like a deer caught in the headlights.

BEAMISH   Kitty was troubled. I couldn't push her over the edge.

EMILY   Kitty had you wrapped around her little finger.

BEAMISH   She had all those pills, clinics, and doctors.

EMILY   And I had God.

BEAMISH   Right.

EMILY   Which most people think is a joke. A crutch. But if it's a crutch, why kick it? I love my faith. But the Bible doesn't keep you warm at night. I'm sorry, God, but I am in pain and it isn't fair. He's dead. You killed him and it isn't fair.

BEAMISH   Emily.

                 BEAMISH moves to comfort her but she moves away.

EMILY   I went to your funeral. You know that. And I sat in the back with the other employees. And no one suspected. Nobody knew.

BEAMISH   Kitty knew.

EMILY   Kitty said, "Oh yes, you're the secretary with the spelling problems, aren't you, dear? So glad you could come." I wanted to smack her. I wanted to shout, "Who do you think reminded the big lug about your anniversaries, you little toad? Who do you think bought your Christmas gifts?" I wanted to scream, "You don't know what it is to grieve. You put on a show with your big, fake tears, but you're waving goodbye with a VISA card." I wanted to be cruel and ugly and horrible. I wanted her to feel the pain I felt. But mostly I wanted to hold you. I wanted to kiss you goodbye. But I couldn't. We were never alone. All I could do was straighten your tie when no one was looking. You were so fussy about your ties. And it was so crooked. I bet Kitty did it for spite.

BEAMISH   She had reason enough.

EMILY   I miss you so much. I've tried to take care of Junior and keep him safe. He's a good boy. He loves you.

BEAMISH   Bullshit.

EMILY   I can just picture you, looking down at me from some cloud saying "Bullshit." You and your language. I'll bet you make Jesus blush.

BEAMISH   My son hates me.

EMILY   But he loves you, Edgar. I see him staring at your picture when he thinks no one's watching.

BEAMISH   You don't know my son.

EMILY   You don't know your son. You can't like yourself until you know who you are. And you can't know who you are when your father is someone like you. He's just trying to break free, Edgar. That's all. He doesn't mean to hurt you. Good Lord, whiskey is a terrible thing. I'm babbling away and there's nobody here.

BEAMISH   I'm here.

EMILY   I'm alone. But I'm not complaining. I have a good life.

BEAMISH   I miss you, Emily.

EMILY   But I wish... I wish.... Dear God, you've given me so much. But the one thing I want is the one thing I can't have. I want him. I want him.

EMILY sinks to her knees and begins to cry.

BEAMISH   I'm here.

BEAMISH moves behind her, sinks to his knees, and holds her tenderly. She cannot feel it.

EMILY   I want to feel him holding me.

BEAMISH   *(gently)* I'm here. I'm here.

EMILY   I want him not to be hurt. I want him not to be angry.

BEAMISH   I'm not.

EMILY   But I want him to know I'm a human being. I want him to know I feel and hurt and rage and hate and love. I miss him so desperately. Please God, please. Wherever you are, if you are—please let him know that I love him.

BEAMISH   I'm here. I know.

EMILY   Please let him know.

BEAMISH   I love you, too.

EMILY wipes her eyes and gets up as if he isn't there.

EMILY   *(wiping her eyes; to herself)* Aren't I the proper fool. I've lived your life for daydreams.

BEAMISH   Emily?

EMILY   I'm an old boozer, that's what I am. As if anyone cares for a Baptist prude.

BEAMISH   I do. Emily? *(EMILY begins straightening the desk.)* Emily?

> *Enter WICHITA on a crutch, his nose in a bloody bandage. The crutch is largely for show. He enjoys waving it for effect.*

WICHITA   We are wounded. Slain. No. Don't bother to help us. Who cares about these old broken bones? They stoned St. Stephen, pierced the heart of St. Sebastian, and crucified Our Lord. Us, they punch in the nose. But we give thanks. Yea, it is our privilege to mortify our flesh for the greater glory of God. *(shouting)* Syphilitic larvae! May they feast on diseased parrot droppings and chew the excrement of parasitic worms!

EMILY   Care for a seat?

WICHITA   *(gives her a look and drops into the chair; philosophically)* Ah well. "Vengeance is mine," sayeth the Lord. We can't wait. For we shall be in Paradise and they'll be off burning in Hell. What fun.

> *WICHITA pulls a huge chunk of wall hanging from his robe, on the theme of St. Sebastian. He proceeds to crochet.*

BEAMISH   I need your help.

WICHITA   We're not in the mood.

EMILY   For what?

WICHITA   This conversation doesn't concern you.

BEAMISH   I want her to see me. I want her to hear me.

WICHITA   She's a Baptist.

BEAMISH   She's in pain. I need to talk to her.

EMILY   *(to WICHITA)* Who are you talking to?

BEAMISH   You're a man of the cloth. You know the spirit world. Help me.

WICHITA   Why should we help you?

BEAMISH   I love her.

WICHITA   Tonight your son burns a van Gogh. And we die. The Holy
Father trusted us and we have failed. The family to whom
we have devoted our life will turn its back on us in hatred
and contempt. We are to be the laughing stock of Rome and
a hideous footnote in history. Why should we worry about
your problems?

EMILY   Are you talking to Edgar?

WICHITA   Don't bother us.

EMILY   You are, aren't you?

WICHITA   Yes.

EMILY   Edgar? Edgar? I didn't mean it. I didn't. Talk to me. Please talk
to me.

BEAMISH   Please. Say something. Help us.

WICHITA   If we do it for you we'd have to do it for everyone.

EMILY   Edgar, why don't you say something? Why don't you talk
to me?

VOICE   *(on Tannoy speaker)* Would Emily Pristable report stage right.
The curtain is rising.

   Distressed, EMILY turns to go.

WICHITA   Wait! Ms. Pristable! *(His eyes flame with inspiration.)*
You want a message from Edgar? We shall give you a message
from Edgar. Edgar wants you to know that he regrets ever
meeting you.

EMILY & BEAMISH
   What?

WICHITA   You are a thorn in his side. A chancre on his soul.

BEAMISH   *(lunging at him)* Liar!

WICHITA   *(looks up from his crocheting, calmly)* One wrong move and
I'll damn you to Hell.

EMILY   You've damned me to Hell already.

WICHITA   He doesn't speak to you because he doesn't want to. In fact, he never wants to see your sorry face again.

EMILY   You're lying.

BEAMISH   You tell him.

EMILY   He loves me.

WICHITA   Then why can't you see him?

EMILY   Don't confuse me. It isn't fair.

WICHITA   He says you betrayed him. You led his son astray.

EMILY   I didn't.

WICHITA   Prove it.

EMILY   How?

WICHITA   Stop him from burning that painting.

EMILY   I can't. I'd destroy the Angel. I'd kill Junior.

WICHITA   Do you want to speak to Edgar?

EMILY   Yes.

WICHITA   Then do what you have to do.

BEAMISH   You don't have to do anything.

WICHITA   You'll be on stage when it happens.

VOICE   (*on Tannoy*) Would Emily Pristable report stage right. The curtain is rising.

EMILY   I've got to go.

WICHITA   It's up to you.

EMILY   (*to the air*) Edgar—be with me?

BEAMISH   Whatever happens.

       EMILY runs off, BEAMISH about to follow.

WICHITA   Stay where you are if you know what's good for you.

BEAMISH   You're a cruel, self-serving, self-satisfied bastard.

WICHITA   We get the job done.

BEAMISH   She's a human being.

WICHITA   Human beings are dust. We serve God, the Father of us all.

BEAMISH   What kind of father brutalizes his children?

WICHITA   Look in the mirror.

BEAMISH   But I want to change. I want to heal the hurt. It can't be too late.

WICHITA   You made your Hell. Live in it.

We hear dim sound of applause from downstairs.

BEAMISH   *(eyes heavenward)* A miracle. Send me a miracle.

ANGEL'S TRUMPET

2M / 1F

It could be successfully argued that Sharon Pollock is the most-accomplished playwright contained within this anthology. She has written over twenty plays, a dozen television scripts, has a multitude of directing credits to her name, has won almost every theatre award (including a GG in 1981 for *Blood Relations*, in 1985 for *Doc*, and nominated in 1986 for *Whiskey Six Cadenza*), scripted several TYA plays, has led workshops, and has spoken on theatre all over the world. Pollock has served as artistic director in several regional theatres across Canada, including a season at the Stratford Festival (which has produced three of her plays), and a term as writer-in-residence at the National Arts Centre. She has been chairperson of the Advisory Arts Panel for the Canada Council for the Arts and head of the Playwrights Colony at the Banff Centre, and started a theatre company in Calgary. She has received four honorary doctorates from Canadian universities. And she is the mother of six children.

Needless to say, *Angel's Trumpet* is not the most widely known of Sharon Pollock's plays; however, it represents two of her most enduring passions, historical subjects and the personal and/or social consequences for individuals—women in particular—who pursue their ambitions. In *Blood Relations*, Pollock adapts the iconic Lizzie Borden story into a daughter's struggle to achieve independence; in the autobiographical play *Doc*, she details the consequences for a daughter of an ambitious father. In *Angel's Trumpet*, Pollock revisits this theme, and historical figures, using the tragic life of Zelda Fitzgerald as a tender vessel, tempest-tost by the ambitions of her famous husband, Scott.

SCOTT	You never believed in me or my writing! *(to RENTON)* Refused to marry me till the publishers' cheques started coming!
ZELDA	I drew sketches of Gatsby till my fingers ached, so you could see the man clear in your mind! "Revisions with Zelda." "Revising with Zelda." Isn't that what you said to Ober and Perkins?
SCOTT	So we collaborate now?
ZELDA	No.
SCOTT	Isn't that what you're saying?
ZELDA	No!
SCOTT	The literary achievement of Scott Fitzgerald is the result of collaboration with his crazy wife, Zelda!
ZELDA	No!
SCOTT	That's what she wants the world to believe!
ZELDA	I contribute!
SCOTT	Nothing!
ZELDA	Something!
SCOTT	Nothing! The money! That's all it ever meant to you. I'm caught in a descending spiral churning out short stories, putting aside major work, and for what?
ZELDA	For another gin and no mix!
SCOTT	For you! To keep you in treatment, that's what!
ZELDA	I don't ask to be treated!
SCOTT	Where you have time and opportunity to indulge yourself on paper while my time is spent grinding out grist for the magazine mill and the movies!
ZELDA	I'm disciplined and I c-concentrate!

SCOTT	You have a manic obsession!
ZELDA	I marshal my f-forces!
SCOTT	A manic obsession! First you think you're a dancer! Now you think you're a writer!
ZELDA	I need to Do Something!
SCOTT	You don't need to Do Something! You just want to Be Someone! There's a difference you know!
	Pause.
ZELDA	I thought I was a salamander once. I thought I could live in fire.
	He tells me I'm nothing. I'm an impediment. An encumbrance.
	I need to find out which of these stories is true.
SCOTT	*(exhausted)* Can't you grasp the simple fact that Scotty needs to be educated and fed? That there is a household, such as it is, to maintain?
ZELDA	*(and she is exhausted)* You're always there.
SCOTT	Now what are you saying?
ZELDA	Scotty.
SCOTT	What about Scotty?
ZELDA	You're there.
SCOTT	Where?
ZELDA	There's no room for me at the table.
SCOTT	What, when we eat? There's plenty of room at the table. Your place is set. Why aren't you in it?
ZELDA	I wanted a boy.
SCOTT	A beautiful little girl. She wanted a boy.
ZELDA	She was born, and I said words. I think that's why he was there, so he could fling a net, pull them in, swallow them whole, and later push them down "Daisy's" throat with his tongue… and

when "Daisy" speaks... words stolen out of my mouth. She's always present tense, and me? Always past, words disappear into air, snatched away, do you know what I mean? I wanted to call her Patricia.

SCOTT   Her name is Frances Scott Fitzgerald.

ZELDA   Pat.

SCOTT   Her name is Scotty.

ZELDA   He's always teaching her something, he's reading her something.

SCOTT   It's what fathers do, Zelda!

ZELDA   *(She begins to turn round and round in the same spot.)* He hires her nannies, oversees her studies, teaches her chess, decides which sport, what class, whose friends, what time, he's a very good father!

SCOTT   She has no mother!

ZELDA   Poor Thing! *(turning faster and faster, pounding the air with her fists)* Pooooor thiiing!

SCOTT   Zelda! *(moving to stop her)*

RENTON   Let her go. Let her go! Leave her.

> SCOTT turns to RENTON. ZELDA will gradually stop on her own.

SCOTT   Let. Her. Go. Let her go…. And where would she like to go, doctor? A public institution? Which will be all I can afford if things aren't resolved!

Would you like to go there, Zelda? That snake pit for crazies?

ZELDA   No, no not— Like an oyster, you know, like an oyster?

SCOTT   *(to RENTON)* See what you've started?

ZELDA   Everything's gone. Those things that you said were inside? They're all gone now. The glorious, glorious Glory? Inside? It's gone. Empty. Shucked from my shell, hollow inside. What do I fill it with now?

SCOTT   *(sits)* Here we go.

ZELDA	Somebody tell me!
SCOTT	That's enough.
ZELDA	The bitterness and the anger inside, can you take that away?
RENTON	Zelda.
ZELDA	And replace it with what, tell me what? You don't know with what! He doesn't know! Nobody knows! *(She retreats.)*
SCOTT	Now… Doctor… Renton, now… you… you will do… you will do as I say.
RENTON	I will do what is called for.
SCOTT	And I will tell you what is called for. Zelda?
RENTON	What is medically called for!
SCOTT	You will back my position. Do you want to know why? *(gently)* Zelda?
ZELDA	*(a spiritual discovery is beginning to fill the "empty inside")* God will come. If you call, He will come.
SCOTT	Is the doctor writing?
ZELDA	I called. You. Yes, yes I did.
SCOTT	Is the doctor writing a book? A book, Zelda, like you told me before?
RENTON	The answer is no.
ZELDA	*(talking to SCOTT, referring to SCOTT as God)* "Do Do" I called you.
SCOTT	Is he writing?
RENTON	We've settled that question!
ZELDA	And they said what does that mean "Dieu Dieu;" why do you call Him that?
SCOTT	Just answer me, Zelda.
RENTON	For God's sake leave her alone!

ZELDA	*(kneeling, clasping SCOTT's hand)* I call you God, and I'm calling you God, and I'm asking you to let me go, Dieu.
SCOTT	Does he run little errands?
RENTON	No.
ZELDA	Please fill me with something. Send voices and visions and You can take all the words!
SCOTT	Did he deliver your novel?
RENTON	The answer is no!
ZELDA	I don't care, you can have them.
SCOTT	Yes, Zelda?
ZELDA	I'll write in tongues and no one will hear.

> *ZELDA begins speaking in tongues, a low murmur, running the words together, pressing SCOTT's hand to her cheek. It's actually a list of the Parisian bars in which SCOTT and she drank.*

Deux Magots Closerie des Lilas Lipp's Coupole Dome Montmartre Select Trianon Ciro's Foyot la Reine Pedauque

SCOTT	She says the answer is yes.
RENTON	Why?
ZELDA	*(continuing to speak under the men's dialogue)* Trianon Ciro's Foyot la Reine Pedauque Bricktop's Zelli's le Perroquet Maxim's Crillon the Ritz Deux Magots Closerie des Lilas Lipp's Coupole Dome Montmartre Select Trianon Ciro's Foyot la Reine Pedauque Bricktop's Zelli's le Perroquet Maxim's Crillon the Ritz Deux Magots Closerie des Lilas Lipp's Coupole Dome Montmartre Select Trianon Ciro's Foyot la Reine Pedauque Bricktop's Zelli's le Perroquet Maxim's Crillon the Ritz Deux Magots Closerie des Lilas Lipp's Coupole
RENTON	Why are you doing this?
SCOTT	*(extricates himself from ZELDA's grasp)* There will be no more of her "artistic expression," most particularly none in the literary field, unless I approve.

RENTON	And control?
SCOTT	Painting. She likes painting. She can paint what she likes. But her literary indulgence is a prelude to breakdown. Is that your analysis, doctor? *(pause)* Or would you prefer to pursue your career in a state-run snake pit, instead of the prestigious and private Phipps clinic?
RENTON	Why?
SCOTT	You say that you listen, but do you actually hear?
RENTON	I can see. Look at her! Look what you're doing!
SCOTT	What I'm doing. What am I doing? I tell you over and over what I am doing and why I am doing it. I am fighting for the Material Survival of the Fitzgerald Ménage, Cracked and Crazed as its Members Might Be!

> *ZELDA's murmur is dying away.*

	Believe that! And… and for the one thing that in the end really matters…. The Writing.
	I am writing! Because I'm a Writer! I am writing a novel!
ZELDA	It's my fault he didn't make the football team at Princeton, I know that!
SCOTT	An intensely personal novel, one in which psychiatry and psychiatric material play a predominant role!
ZELDA	Was never president of the triangle Triangle Club!
SCOTT	She's taken research material belonging to me, didn't you, Zelda?
ZELDA	He never married Ginevra King! Never led his men over hills to kill Huns!
SCOTT	That's how I knew.
ZELDA	My fault!
SCOTT	Knew she was writing and mining the same seam of personal experience and research as I am. Again!
ZELDA	My fault?

SCOTT	Just like before!
ZELDA	*(She's working herself into a violent attack on him, trying to find a way, in self-defence, to penetrate his defences.)* My fault you always feel poor among rich? Not as bright among brilliant?
SCOTT	You promised, after your novel, the publication of which I did not prevent, you promised you would concentrate on your painting!
ZELDA	Is that my fault?!
SCOTT	I want to hear you agree to that today!
ZELDA	Is it my fault you need to be noticed! And to do what you need to do to be noticed, you need to be drunk!
SCOTT	*(to RENTON)* Why can't you see what I'm up against?
ZELDA	Not a nice drunk! A nasty, obnoxious, obstreperous drunk! And then when you're drunk you're unable to write! That is not my fault!
SCOTT	Life with you necessitates drink. It's a means of survival!
ZELDA	I Can write! And I Will write! Because I keep at it and on it and do it! And you cannot forgive me for that!

> She has wounded him. He moves away to get a drink; she follows him, wanting to deal a mortal blow physically and psychologically. He can't get away from her.

Is it my fault your father was nothing!
A failure!
A pretentious and poor Irish clerk!
Who lived off your mother!
Went on discreet Irish binges!
Drunk in the yard!
Trying to play ball with his son!
Falling down drunk!
Neighbours at windows! Laughing! Yes, laughing and pointing and!!

SCOTT	*(grabs her wrists, stopping her physical and verbal assault)* EE-nough!! *(pause)*

The last time you mentioned my father,
I bloodied your nose,
and blackened your eye,
and your sister did go home in a cab.
You hurt me.
I hit you.
I want you to know, that at this moment, you have inflicted no
pain. No Pain, I feel... absolutely No Pain.... None at all.

> *SCOTT releases her wrists, gets his drink. Pause. He takes in
> RENTON. He speaks conversationally almost as if he were
> picking up where a prior friendly and informal conversation
> had left off. He ignores ZELDA.*

You know... I told Edmund once—my friend?—Edmund
Wilson? I told him, near my beginning... before the
beginning... that I had a dream. I wanted Scott Fitzgerald
to be one of the greatest writers that ever lived. I suppose he
thought I was a bit of a fool. A young fool. "One of the greatest
writers that ever lived." I meant it.

I met Zelda.
And we have continued. On.
From there.

Carole Fréchette (1949–)

HELEN'S NECKLACE

Translated by John Murrell

2M / 1F

Carole Fréchette has won honours for her playwriting in both the English- and French-speaking world. For *Le Collier d'Hélène (Helen's Necklace)* she received, during the first year of its publication, France's Sony Labou Tansi Award and the Prix de la Francophonie. In 2002, she received a GG nomination for *Jean et Béatrice* and won Canada's richest theatre award, the Siminovitch Prize. Previous awards include a 1995 GG for *Les Quatre morts de Marie* (which also won a 1998 Chalmers) and two other GG nominations. She has also made a French translation of Colleen Wagner's *The Monument*, the second scene in this anthology.

It is in keeping with Fréchette's international reputation that the first production of *Le Collier d'Hélène (Helen's Necklace)* was in Beirut, Lebanon. Although the setting of *Helen's Necklace* is not specifically mentioned, it likely takes place in the aftermath of the 1982 conflict between Lebanon and Israel. This protracted, devastating war has been an engaging subject for more than one playwright during the decades covered in this anthology (it also inspired Wajdi Mouawad's plays *Tideline* and *Scorched*) and obviously struck a chord with many Canadians.

Helen is a Western academic attending an international conference. She tours the city and loses a cheap, plastic necklace that has only sentimental value. As the play opens, the distraught Helen hires Nabil, a taxi driver, to take her on a rather desultory tour of the places she thinks she may have lost her necklace. In the process she meets, one after the other, four local citizens whose lives have all been profoundly changed by the war. By play's end, these encounters have a similar effect on Helen and the audience.

NABIL   *El bahr kbiir.* Which way, Miss Helen?

HELEN   That way. *Yalla!*

NABIL   *Yalla!*

HELEN   We depart again. It's so hot. The sun beats down on the
Mercedes. Suddenly I think of my colleagues. Home again in
their cool Northern country. What must they have thought
when they got my note? "Dear Colleagues, you should leave
without me. I've decided to stay on for a while in order to…."
In order to? What did I write after that? I can't recall. They
must have been astounded. "Helen has lost interest in us,"
René would say, "She's fallen in love with an Arab prince."
The others would laugh at that. "Helen is so secretive. She's
been lost in thought ever since we got here." "Everybody's lost
in thought at these conferences," René would say, "We're paid
to be lost in thought." And everybody would laugh again. But
that morning at the airport, they must have felt anxious, they
tried calling my hotel room, but nobody answered, and their
flight was already boarding. So they left. Where are we now?
A different neighbourhood. Was I ever here before? I can't
recall. "Look all around down there, think about your necklace,
and say to yourself, 'I will never find it again. Never. *Abadan.*'"
We're driving alongside a wall which encloses a small town.
A separate town within the city. Where is the sea? A man on
the sidewalk waits for a break in the traffic so he can cross.
We pass by. Suddenly my heart is pounding. Oh my God, isn't
that—? That's him, isn't it? I'm sure it is. *(to NABIL)* Stop!
Stop here!

NABIL   Here, please? Not the sea here.

HELEN   I don't care. Stop! Wait for me here, Nabil. Please.

NABIL   Not here, please.

HELEN   I understand, you can't park here. Go around the block.
(She gestures.) Go around a block or two, and come back
here to pick me up. Understand?

NABIL   Here, please?

HELEN   Exactly. Right here. In ten minutes. Ten. He drives away. But did he understand? I have no idea. I push my way through the crowd, looking for that man—where is he? There, I see him, but he's walking so fast. *(She shouts.)* Please! Wait just a moment. Please!

　　　　　THE MAN turns around.

THE MAN   Me?

HELEN   Don't you recognize me? We first saw each other not long ago. It must have been around here somewhere. I can't recall. I was lost. I asked you for directions.

THE MAN   I think you are mistaken.

HELEN   No, no, I approached you, and you were so kind, so polite. You looked at me, and you smiled. It made you smile, a woman like me lost in a city like this. We talked for a minute or two. You asked me where I came from, and I told you about my cold Northern country, where the snow comes down in big white flakes. Then you complimented me on my necklace. Remember? I was wearing a fragile necklace of little white pearls, so light and delicate. You said, "Your necklace is lovely." And you touched it with your fingertips. And I… it seemed wonderful and strange to me, your fingers on my throat, and then we looked into one another's eyes and—

THE MAN   And?

HELEN   And… I have lost it since then, my necklace, and I've been wondering if… if maybe it slipped off and fell at your feet, just when you touched.… Or if it could have fallen into one of your boots, and that evening when you took off your boots, maybe you discovered it.

THE MAN   You have lost your necklace?

HELEN   Exactly, and I was wondering if—

THE MAN   Look at me. I have lost my place. My place on earth. Maybe it fell into one of your shoes? I have lost the place where I can stand and say, "This is mine." Did you happen to discover it

when you took off your shoes, that place where I can stand?
And I have also lost: "Some day, I will have a house with
a garden." And: "Some day, I will travel to a cold Northern
land where snow falls in big flakes." And: "Some day, my
children will have real jobs, they will be doctors or teachers or
truck drivers, they will have houses with gardens and they will
have a place on this earth." And I have lost: "Look all around,
my son, my daughter, this is the earth and it belongs to you.
Take it up, explore it, transform it. Make of it what you will."
Did that, perhaps, slip into one of your shoes, my children's
future? And I have also lost the ability to cry out—maybe you
found it inside one of your shoes, my ability to cry out, to beat
my fist against the wall. Did you happen to find my cry in your
purse, in your blouse, in your throat? Open your mouth.

HELEN I don't want—

THE MAN Open your mouth.

> *HELEN opens her mouth.*

Go ahead. You cry out. I want to see. Cry out: "We cannot
go on living like this. We cannot go on." Shout it.

HELEN I'm sorry, I must have been mistaken—

THE MAN *(seizing her by the shoulders)* Shout it! Cry out!

HELEN *(quietly, hesitantly)* We cannot go on living like this.

THE MAN Louder, much louder!

HELEN *(louder, crying out)* We cannot go on living like this. We cannot
go on living like this.

THE MAN *(shaking her)* Louder!

HELEN *(crying out as loud as she can)* We cannot go on living like this!
We cannot go on living like this! Stop! Please, stop!

> *He lets her go. She stops shouting.*
>
> *Trembling, she looks into his eyes.*

THE MAN   Forgive me. I did not mean to. I do not know what possessed me. Today is one of my dark days. There are days of light when I manage to forget that I have been walled up inside a camp since the day I was born. I look at my children and they look beautiful to me, I get busy, I eat and drink, I make use of the day which God has given us, I live life like you or like anybody else. But then there are days of darkness, when I see only the wall which walls us in, our houses piled on top of one another, the lack of space and privacy, the filth, the ugliness, and I say to myself, over and over for hours, "This is my only life, I will never have another, this is my only life, and I will live it here," and then when I see people like you walking down the street, people from somewhere else who do not give a damn about my despair—

HELEN   We do give a damn. But we can't—we can't seem to do anything. What can we do?

THE MAN   I do not know. Maybe, when you go home to your own country, to that little place which belongs to you, sometimes you should say, "We cannot go on living like this." When you go to a party with your friends, when you are drinking wine, when you look out the window at your white city, so quiet and so organized, say these words, even if no one understands, even if you do not remember yourself where the phrase comes from, because it is from so long ago, from so far away, from the other side of the earth. Say it.

HELEN   We cannot go on living like this.

THE MAN   Promise me.

>   *Pause.*

HELEN   I do. I promise you. *(She starts out.)*

THE MAN   Wait. You said you had lost something?

HELEN   No, nothing. It's not important.

THE MAN   Did you say a necklace?

HELEN   Yes, a necklace. But I was mistaken. You're not the man I asked for directions.

THE MAN   No, I was not that man. But you can ask me now, if you wish.

HELEN   It's no longer necessary. Here's my taxi.

Morris Panych (1952–)

GIRL IN THE GOLDFISH BOWL

2M / 1F

Like many of his contemporaries, Morris Panych attended university in the seventies, graduating from UBC with a BFA in creative writing. He is the West Coast's most prolific playwright (having created over twenty-five plays) and has a successful acting and directing career as well. In the latter categories, he has won the Jessie Richardson Theatre Award, Vancouver's "Jessie," fourteen times. He has also been nominated six times for Toronto's Dora Mavor Moore Award, three times for the Chalmers Award, and twice received the Governor General's Literary Award for Drama, first in 1994 for *The Ends of the Earth* and again in 2004 for *Girl in the Goldfish Bowl*. This drama also won a Dora in the year of its first production, 2003. Only in his fifties, Panych's imaginative and forceful blend of the absurd with the tragic, of fantasy with reality, is a force in Canadian theatre and will be for years to come.

The girl in the goldfish bowl is Iris, a precocious ten-year-old whose charming turns of logic illuminate her dysfunctional world for the audience. These are best evidenced in this excerpt by her opening monologue. The play is a flashback; Iris is experiencing "the last few days of her childhood," and as such, *Girl in the Goldfish Bowl* is a coming-of-age story. Although her awakening to the harsh realities of the adult world are distorted like light through water by her delightful imagination, she is constantly reminded of the watery limits of her little bowl that is her family. Thus, Panych has set Iris in a house, "like a place submerged underwater at high tide." The playful, comic surface of her childhood is reduced by her deeper realization of the dysfunctional, adult world.

The family's new boarder, Mr. Lawrence, bears to Iris an eerie resemblance to her dead goldfish, Amahl (so named because he was purchased at "a mall"). It is this imagery that cleverly introduces her fractured world to the audience. As in memory and dream, characters enter and exit seemingly out of nowhere, timed to the extravagancies of Iris's imagination. Mr. Lawrence's entrance, and later the reappearance of Owen, her father, are such events, but it is in this part of the play the audience gets its clearest portrait of the world according to Iris.

OWEN exits. IRIS is alone. She digs out a secret box of old photos.

IRIS   My mother's only true love was an Australian motorcyclist named Arnie, who was killed in France, in the line of duty, January 17, 1944. So every year, on the seventeenth day of January, my mother goes down at twilight, and sits at the end of the pier, looking southeast. She's never really loved my father.

SYLVIA appears in a wedding veil, sighs.

But when he came back from the war in a stretcher, she decided to marry him anyway.

SYLVIA evaporates.

Now and again we take in boarders because my father can't really work. Once, a Chinese man lived with us who was a Buddhist. Every day he scaled salmon in twelve-hour shifts, for two whole years, so he could bring his wife from China. But she never came. And so, one day, he left the house at eleven p.m., and he wandered down to the arbutus tree and he sat down and just died. It was a medical mystery. We went to his funeral and lit firecrackers. After, my father got me a goldfish, which I named Amahl because that's where we bought him. Every evening, my mother and my father would sit, and read, sometimes for hours and hours, and every once in a while, my mother would look up at Amahl, turning his circles, and my father would look over at her, and they would both take a deep breath, as if they were coming up for air. From where I sat, on the other side of the bowl, it seemed like life might just go on like this forever. Swimmingly. And that's how things were on our street until this morning. On October the twenty-second, in the Year of Our Lord nineteen hundred and sixty-two, Amahl passed away quietly. This afternoon, as the president of the United States was delivering his ultimatum to the Russians, my mother decided to leave my father forever. She packed her bags and she said goodbye, but as she was leaving she stumbled and fell and broke her wrist. The doctor came and he said it wasn't serious, but he doesn't know the whole story. Now my father sits beside her bed, never once closing his eyes, never sleeping, but dreaming about Paris all the same. Because one day, he hopes to take my mother there. And on that day, he thinks she will finally love him. Owing to the alignment of the streets. Would you like a cocktail?

LAWRENCE
What have you got?

Mr. LAWRENCE appears out of nowhere.

IRIS   Crème de menthe. It's quite lovely. Or there's Chartreuse.

LAWRENCE
Do you have—ginger ale? I don't mean ginger ale. I mean—water?

IRIS   Are you afraid of communists?

LAWRENCE
Just—dogs. And—what?

Beat.

IRIS   We don't normally get overnight visitors at this time of year.

Beat.

Are you a poet by any chance?

LAWRENCE
Why?

IRIS   You just seem that way.

LAWRENCE
Yeah?

IRIS   If there's an atomic war, everybody will have to eat canned spaghetti for a whole month. Imagine. Mr. DaSilva says the world is divided, now, because everyone within themselves is divided. But he's bound to say that sort of thing because he's Portuguese. Besides, he's blind, so it's allowed. It's like when an Italian kisses your hand. If an ordinary person did that, you'd just think it was creepy. You're very handsome, you know. But in an unconventional way.

Looking at him more closely.

You don't really have any earlobes to speak of.

LAWRENCE

No?

IRIS

I can make you a Manhattan if you like.

LAWRENCE

Did you say how... how old you were?

IRIS

Almost eleven. Mr. DaSilva says I have a very old soul, though. Do you believe in reincarnation, by the way?

Miss Rose thinks that a human being is the lowest thing you can become. She's our one and only boarder at the moment. She works at the cannery, and she keeps the temperature in her room about a million degrees. I hate to say it, but she smells just a little like fresh halibut. Even though she has about six lavender baths a day. She soaks forever and she never, ever drains the tub. This is my father's drafting table. Do you like it? It's made completely out of oak.

LAWRENCE

Congratulations.

Curious beat.

IRIS

He studied physics for two years at the university. But after he came home from overseas he couldn't really do much of anything. He's a drug addict now. Once, on April Fool's Day, he pretended to hang himself. And he nearly did.

Beat.

Are you at all familiar with the work of Nikolai Lobachevsky?

LAWRENCE

Yes. No.

IRIS

Well, he introduced the idea that two parallel lines could intersect, which is a constant source of fascination for my father, but no one else. If he brings up the subject, just do what my mother does and pretend you smell something burning in the kitchen. I'm a Buddhist, by the way. Sister Anamelda says that Catholicism is completely incompatible with Buddhism, even though they both have nuns. She has a very large boil on her eyelid, so even when her eye is closed it looks like it's still open. You wonder why God would do something so ugly and cruel to such a religious, old woman. But who knows. Maybe He actually has a sense of humour. Miss Rose doesn't believe in God at all. Which is extraordinary, because she's my godmother. My father, by the way, doesn't even believe in a soul. What about you, Mr. Lawrence?

LAWRENCE
I've been to hell.

IRIS
That must have been interesting.

LAWRENCE
I don't know what I believe.

IRIS
That wouldn't necessarily make you an atheist; just indecisive. That's a ten-letter word.

LAWRENCE
My hands feel like they're not attached.

IRIS
They seem to be. I hope you're warm enough. I can get you a blanket if you like. Are you aware that you have practically no hair on your legs whatsoever. I believe that's a sign of intelligence.

LAWRENCE
Not if you shave them it isn't.

IRIS
I never heard of a man shaving his legs before. I'll have to write that down in my diary. I'm keeping a complete record of everything.

Beat.

LAWRENCE
Why?

IRIS   It's my father's idea, actually. He says that I ask too many questions. He says I should just write them down, because at some later date, I'll be able to answer them all myself. Tell me a little more about hell. Did you happen to see Father Wallace? He was our parish priest. He was quite controversial, but he died of emphysema.

LAWRENCE
Where did you say your dad was, ma'am?

IRIS   Well, like I told you—

Appearing from upstairs.

OWEN   Right here.

Beat.

IRIS   Look. A perfect stranger.

LAWRENCE
Sir.

OWEN   What's—going on?

IRIS   I found him on the beach.

OWEN   No kidding?

LAWRENCE
Yeah. I'm—I—I'm—

IRIS   This is Mr.Lawrence. His hands feel like they're not attached.

OWEN   What are you doing in that—bathrobe?

IRIS   It's yours.

OWEN   Is it?

IRIS   It's quite the story.

OWEN   Why don't you let him tell it.

IRIS   My father wants me to take a vow of silence.

OWEN   No one likes a ten-year-old with an opinion.

IRIS   Especially a more interesting one.

OWEN   So. What's the, uh—what's the story?

LAWRENCE
             Your daughter took all my clothes, sir.

OWEN   Sorry. Headache. Sorry. She, she what?

IRIS   He's looking for a room to rent.

OWEN   Is that right?

LAWRENCE
             I—might be.

OWEN   Not sure?

IRIS   He's a poet.

OWEN   A poet.

LAWRENCE
             I just—seem like one.

IRIS   And he's been to hell.

OWEN   What have you done with his clothes, Iris?

IRIS   They're wet.

OWEN   Where's my prescription got to? Hell?

IRIS   I believe you took them all.

OWEN   And why are your clothes wet? Is that something I care
             to know?

LAWRENCE
             I fell in the water.

OWEN   Oh, is that right?

LAWRENCE
             It's very foggy out, sir.

OWEN   Uh huh?

IRIS   I heard a splash.

LAWRENCE
             Suddenly, everything disappeared underneath me. It was—

OWEN   Would you mind not following me around the room, Iris?

IRIS   My father is a recluse.

OWEN   So you needed a place to stay? Is that—? Is—is—that—?

IRIS   We can put you in Mr. Lowell's old room. He ran off with the Avon lady.

OWEN   That, of course, is not true. Excuse me. I have to sit down. Sorry. You seem like a very nice—man, Mr. Lawrence. A very nice, very straightforward sort of, soaking wet sort of—and a poet no less. That's—

LAWRENCE
            Not—

OWEN   But we can't have you staying here, I'm afraid. We—we just— we can't. Find me an Aspirin. Sorry. We don't take boarders anymore. It's—it's—

LAWRENCE
            I thought that might be the case.

OWEN   Yes. It's—yes—the case. Sorry.

IRIS   What about Miss Rose?

OWEN   She's—hardly a boarder. She's a family friend. Well, friend is a—she's a long-time—I shouldn't even say resident. That sounds a little—

IRIS   She finds my father sexually attractive. Which is extraordinary.

OWEN   You know the rule about using words that have more letters than your age.

IRIS   *(to Mr. LAWRENCE)* I'm not allowed to say "senectitude" until after my birthday.

OWEN   Won't that be delightful?

            Beat.

            Even if we did have room, which we don't, really—my wife isn't well. She's not, well she's—she's—well, she's just—she's— how should I put this—she's—

IRIS   Not well.

OWEN   She's—thank you, Iris. Not well.

LAWRENCE

        I heard she fell—down—the stairs and—broke her wrist.

OWEN   It's actually a little more serious than that.

LAWRENCE

        Oh, I'm sorry.

OWEN   It's a compound fracture. Iris, I wonder if you could stop
        rolling your eyes to the back of your head for a minute and go
        and see if Mr. Lawrence's clothes are dry. He must be awfully,
        awfully anxious to get out of here. Are you?

LAWRENCE

        I was enjoying the visit.

OWEN   Oh.

LAWRENCE

        She was telling me about her goldfish.

IRIS   Isn't it tragic?

OWEN   Yes. We were all pretty—broken up about it.

LAWRENCE

        I guess he was quite the fish, then. Influential.

OWEN   What?

LAWRENCE

        What?

IRIS   I don't think it's a coincidence that ever since he was flushed
        down the toilet, American warships have been steaming their
        way towards Havana.

LAWRENCE

        Stranger things have happened.

OWEN   Have they?

LAWRENCE

        Have—haven't they?

OWEN   Look; if you don't mind, Mr. Lawrence, I wonder if you could get out of my—bathrobe, please. It's—*(Mr. LAWRENCE complies)*—and back into your own things if they're—hold it—what are you—? Not here. Please. *(Covering Mr. LAWRENCE again)* Are you out of your—? This is—

LAWRENCE
You said—

OWEN   I didn't mean—for God's sake! Please! Put them—please.

LAWRENCE
Sorry.

OWEN   Good grief.

IRIS   My father is a bit of a prude.

OWEN   I'm not.

LAWRENCE
I understand.

IRIS   Personally, I find the sight of male genitals extremely disappointing.

OWEN   That's the last time I let anybody take you to a livestock show.

LAWRENCE
You and me, we were in school together, or something.

OWEN   What?

LAWRENCE
Have I seen you before?

OWEN   I doubt it. What are you—?

LAWRENCE
What?

OWEN   —talking about?

LAWRENCE
Sometimes, I recognize people I haven't—you know?—met.

OWEN   Uh huh.

LAWRENCE

It's just that—that—sometimes even the strangest, what do you call them?— surroundings seem—to—to—yeah—or, or I find myself remembering things as they're—as— But I think that's just—a collision of molecules, like possibilities. Don't you? Or maybe an electrical impulse or something. Wires connecting the front part of the brain and—and uh—and I, I don't recall the rest.

Beat.

IRIS

I think you'll make a scintillating guest, Mr. Lawrence.

Colleen Murphy (1954–)

THE DECEMBER MAN
(L'HOMME DE DÉCEMBRE)

2M / 1F

Colleen Murphy is a filmmaker and playwright who grew up among the francophone population of northern Ontario. *The December Man (L'homme de décembre)* won the 2007 GG for Drama, the Carol Bolt Award, and an Enbridge playRites Award. An earlier work, *Beating Heart Cadaver*, was nominated for a 1999 Governor General's Literary Award and a Chalmers Award. Over the last fifteen years Murphy has also produced numerous award-winning short films. She was married to renowned Canadian documentary director, Allan King, who passed away in June, 2009.

The December Man draws a clear picture of the human impact of tragic, public events covered in numbing repetition in our daily media. Murphy's drama is the story of a working-class family, Benoît, Kathleen, and their only son, Jean, an engineering student around whom they have built their dreams. A student at Montreal's École Polytechnique, Jean witnesses the Montreal Massacre of December 1989 when fourteen female students are murdered by Marc Lépine as they attend an engineering lecture. Jean cannot shake the trauma of what he has seen—to the point where, two years later, he hangs himself in the basement of his parents' home. The play begins a few months after his death as Benoît and Kathleen, who now realize they, themselves, have nothing left to live for, prepare their own mutual suicide. Structurally, each scene of the play marks a point going back in time until the audience witnesses the day of the Massacre in the last of the eight scenes. Scene six is the best expression of Jean's anguish over the event as he struggles to explain his feelings of guilt and rage to his mother, Kathleen, some six months after the slayings.

July 1990.

It's dark. JEAN lays on the couch in his pyjamas. The television is on but the sound is turned down. Light and shadows from the screen flicker across JEAN's sleeping face.

Hovering like a ghost in the background, the structure—without the Plexiglas square—leans only very slightly to one side.

Without opening his eyes JEAN begins to scream… a high-pitched scream that starts softly then builds into a frightened howl, like a tenor going into shock when he hits high C.

After a moment, KATHLEEN enters in her nightgown.

KATE   Jean, Jean—

JEAN   Oh oh oh oh…

KATE   What's the matter?

             JEAN wakes up—panicked, frightened.

JEAN   …run down the escalator oh oh oh oh oh run—

KATE   You all right?

JEAN   …RUN!

KATE   Jean… Jean?

JEAN   …oh oh oh oh—

KATE   JEAN.

JEAN   …yeah, yeah… sorry, Ma.

KATE   Scared me half to death. Went into your room and you weren't there.

JEAN   Came out to watch TV.

KATE   Another nightmare?

             He nods his head heavily, yes.

JEAN	…oh, oh, oh…
KATE	Shhhh. I'll make you some hot chocolate.
JEAN	It's too hot, Ma.
KATE	Ice water.
JEAN	No.
KATE	I made special ice water with pieces of lemon in it.
JEAN	Oh, my head feels… loaded.

> BENOÎT *saunters into the room wearing only pyjama bottoms.*

BENOÎT	What's all the commotion?
KATE	Nightmares again.
BENOÎT	*(to JEAN)* You okay now, Jean?
JEAN	Yeah P'pa.
BENOÎT	You sure?
JEAN	My head aches…
BENOÎT	Hotter than hell in here.
KATE	All the windows are open. Tomorrow's gonna be even hotter.
BENOÎT	If Nelson's would install friggin' air conditioning least I'd be cool during the day. Living in their air-conditioned mansions with maids and martinis and friggin' limousines, but oh no, they can't find the cash to put in AC—management says the fans give cool ventilation year around—cool, for sure, when it's twenty below—*calisse*.
KATE	You want some ice water?
BENOÎT	Eh?
KATE	I made ice water with pieces of lemon floating in it—it'll cool you off.
BENOÎT	Okay.

She exits into the kitchen… a light goes on.

They got air conditioning over at Provigo?

JEAN   Yeah.

BENOÎT   Lucky you. I'm gonna lose five pounds just from sweating.

JEAN   You can have the little fan in my room.

BENOÎT   Ah, that's hardly a breath of air.

JEAN   Go ahead—take it. I'm not that hot.

BENOÎT   When I got polio, kids they teased me 'cause I couldn't do sports. Had bad dreams, too—dreamt I was crippled, couldn't run from people chasing me. I hated doing the special exercises—hurt like hell, but the more I did them, the less they hurt.

> *The kitchen light goes off. KATE enters with a glass of ice water and gives it to BENOÎT.*

…time, eh. Time makes things a bit better. You get some sleep now, eh—good night.

JEAN   Take the fan from my room, P'pa.

BENOÎT   …keep it. *(indicates his lemon drink)* I got this to cool me off.

> *BENOÎT lumbers out of the room and exits stage left.*

KATE   Sure you don't want a nice cool glass of ice water—

JEAN   Ma, I'm sure.

KATE   You gonna watch TV or go back to bed?

JEAN   Do you know what I dream about sometimes?

KATE   What?

JEAN   That no one died.

KATE   Eh?

JEAN   It's a special dream but it starts the same way—he comes in and says, "Everyone stop everything," but everybody ignores him until he fires at the ceiling. At first I think it's a scary

joke... then he says, "Separate—girls on the left, guys on the
right." No one even moves till he shouts, and then the guys,
we go over to the right side where the door is. He waves the
women to the back left corner. Then he says, "Okay—guys
leave, women stay." There's nine women and about forty-five
guys and two professors... so we leave the room and a few of
us stand out in the hall... we hear the guy talking and a woman
talking then bam bam bam... but in the special dream I...
I run back into the classroom and he's standing there, his back
to me, I could see the women bunched up against the wall,
moaning and... ah... I was so scared 'cause I never open my
mouth in class—even when I don't understand something
I just sit there praying someone else will ask the question,
but suddenly I hear someone shout STOP. At first I think it's
a professor who walked in behind me, or a policeman, but it's
me, I'm shouting at the guy and he swings around and fires
and I veer to one side and I say PUT IT DOWN, but he just keeps
firing so I take a bullet in the leg, another in the side of my
head, then calculate that the only way to stop the guy is tackle
him—he's only about five-foot ten, skinny, maybe a hundred
and fifty—so I jump him and his eyes open wide and he runs
out of the room and I'm screaming to the guys out in the hall
to stop him... then... then I start sprouting extra arms so
I scoop up the wounded women until they're all in my arms
and I run out and down the corridor, covered in blood,
running behind him screaming YOU FUCKING COCK SUCKING—

KATE	Jean—
JEAN	MURDERING FUCK PIG SAVAGE—
KATE	Jean, stop it—
JEAN	I don't know where all these extra arms are coming from, Ma, but I keep scooping up women, lifting them, holding onto them for dear life until I can hardly move, and I'm drowning in their blood but I stagger outside and get them to the ambulances in time and no one died, Ma... then I wake up.
KATE	...*mon petit* Jean...
JEAN	That's what I most hate, Ma.

KATE	What?
JEAN	That he was so angry and I was so afraid… I was a tiny, frightened insect scurrying down the escalator—someone should squish me.
KATE	Shhhh—don't say that.
JEAN	Squish me, Ma. Break my spine.
KATE	You did what you could, Jean.
JEAN	I didn't do anything—nothing.
KATE	You phoned 9-1-1.
JEAN	Yeah, after I ran out of the classroom and before I ran out of the building.
KATE	Everyone else ran!
JEAN	That doesn't make it okay!
KATE	It's not okay but what else you gonna do when a crazy's running around with a gun shooting people. This guy I heard on TV, he said ordinary people aren't expected to be heroes in those situations. He said okay—people panic, they freeze or they run—if you froze you prob'ly would have been killed.
JEAN	That's not the point, Ma—point is no one tried to stop him.
KATE	The point is you're still alive.
JEAN	It's not enough to still be alive!
KATE	Yes, it is—you can build buildings and hospitals and churches—
JEAN	Those women will never build anything!
	Silence.
	Ma.
KATE	What?
JEAN	Maybe I'm dead, too.
KATE	Eh?
JEAN	Maybe I didn't get to the ambulance in time.

KATE   Don't talk crazy.

JEAN   He killed me, Ma.

KATE   Your father quit smoking New Year's and it's still hard for him. He sweats, gets up at night crying, he suffers at work 'cause the guys they tease him but he takes it one day at a time—that's what you have to do.

JEAN   Please could I take karate lessons?

KATE   We don't have the money for stuff like that—don't keep asking me.

JEAN   I'll save up my allowance plus use some money from work.

KATE   That money you earn at Provigo is for next year's tuition.

JEAN   But I have to be prepared for when it happens again.

KATE   It'll never happen again.

JEAN   I want it to happen again—and when Marc fuckin' Lépine comes bursting into class I'll have muscles and reflexes... and guts. I left those women once but next time I'll stand and fight—girls on one side, mice on the other, girls on one side, chickens on the other, you monsters get on that side and stay absolutely still or I'll yank your fucking faces off—

KATE   Calm down or my heart's gonna start beating too fast.

JEAN   I ran out of the classroom and I ran and ran, then I missed the bus and figured that was a sign for me to turn back but I was cold so I got on the Metro at Côte-Sainte-Catherine and decided I'd just go one stop then get off at Plamondon and go back to the school but I went right past Plamondon, past Namur, past De la Savane, and when I got off at Du Collège I automatically started walking down Ste. Croix. I kept telling myself to turn around turn around turn around but I was shaking so I ran along Rue Hodge, then turned onto Rue Petit and... *(begins to weep)* ...I left them all to die.

She puts her arms around him and he snuggles into her breast. She begins to hum a lullaby. Her voice is thin and off pitch but she hums with a determination to soothe her son's turmoil.

Ma?

KATE   Yes, Jean.

JEAN   They're following me.

KATE   Who?

JEAN   The women. They're following me.

Blackout.

PART THREE

Scenes for Four or Five

GOODNIGHT DESDEMONA (GOOD MORNING JULIET)

2M / 2F

Actor, playwright, and novelist, Ann-Marie MacDonald is a Canadian cultural icon. Her multi-faceted talent has been widely recognized. As an actor, she has won a Gemini Award (*Where the Spirit Lives*, 1989); her first solo play, *Goodnight Desdemona (Good Morning Juliet)* (1989), won a Dora Mavor Moore Award, the Chalmers Award, and the Governor General's Literary Award (1990). More recently, she has turned her hand to fiction and won a Commonwealth Prize (1997), the Dartmouth Literary Award, and has garnered two Giller Prize nominations for her bestsellers, *Fall On Your Knees* (1996) and *As The Crow Flies* (2003). She also has been a CBC television host and journalist. Her most recent play, *Belle Moral*, was staged in 2005 at the Shaw Festival (remounted in 2008) and directed by her partner, Alisa Palmer. They were married in 2003 and now share a house and a new baby girl in Toronto.

Goodnight Desdemona (Good Morning Juliet) has been described, not unfairly, by Craig Walker as "a witty, postmodernist comedy about a young female professor who enters and alters the patriarchal worlds of Shakespeare's tragedies." MacDonald redesigns Shakespeare's tragic females by throwing the timid Constance Ledbelly, a Queen's University assistant professor, into a play-length reverie. Inspired by her feminist doctoral thesis that Shakespeare's two great tragedies, *Othello* and *Romeo and Juliet*, are really revisions of earlier comedies, Constance tries to rework the dramas from the inside out by reminding the famous female leads first-hand that they have less tragic options.

After rescuing Desdemona from Iago's scheme, Constance time travels to Verona to prevent Juliet from meeting her end, only to become herself the comic object of desire for both hot-blooded, young lovers. Although Constance cannot save her heroines from jealousy or lust, she does experience a redirection of her own life, and thus her romp is a vastly entertaining voyage of self-discovery. This scene is Constance's first, fanciful entrance into her version of *Othello*.

OTHELLO's citadel at Cyprus.

OTHELLO and IAGO reprise the end of the "Handkerchief Scene." Desdemona's "strawberry-spotted" handkerchief hangs out the back of IAGO's hose.

IAGO
Tell me but this:
Have you not sometimes seen a handkerchief
spotted with strawberries in your wife's hand?

OTHELLO
I gave her such a one; 'twas my first gift.

IAGO
I know not that; but such a handkerchief—
I am sure it was your wife's—did I today
see Cassio wipe his beard with.

OTHELLO
If it be that—

IAGO
If it be that, or any that was hers,
It speaks against her with the other proofs.

> *CONSTANCE's head peeks out from behind an arras.*

OTHELLO
Had Desdemona forty-thousand lives!
One is too poor, too weak for my revenge.
Damn her, lewd minx! O, damn her! Damn her, O!
I will chop her into messes! Cuckold me!

IAGO
O, 'tis foul in her.

OTHELLO
With mine officer!

IAGO
That's fouler.

OTHELLO
Get me some poison, Iago, this night.

IAGO
Do it not with poison.

> *IAGO hands a pillow to OTHELLO.*

Strangle her in bed.

CONSTANCE
No!

Both OTHELLO and IAGO turn and stare at her, amazed.

Um… you're about to make a terrible mistake… m'Lord.

Shocked, and at a loss for words to explain her statement, CONSTANCE gathers her courage and timidly approaches IAGO.

Excuse me, please.

She plucks the handkerchief from IAGO's hose and gives it to OTHELLO.

OTHELLO   Desdemona's handkerchief! *(to IAGO)* Which thou didst say she gave to Cassio!

IAGO   Did I say that? What I meant to say—

OTHELLO   *O-o-o! I see that nose of thine, but not that dog I shall throw it to!*

IAGO   My Lord, I can explain—

CONSTANCE

Omigod, what have I done?

She grabs the handkerchief from OTHELLO and tries unsuccessfully to stuff it back into IAGO's pocket.

Look, just forget you ever saw me here, okay?!

She grabs the pillow and offers it to OTHELLO.

Here.

OTHELLO ignores the pillow and proceeds to bind and threaten IAGO.

(aside) I've wrecked a masterpiece. I've ruined the play,
I've turned Shakespeare's *Othello* to a farce.
O Jesus, they've got swords! And this is Cyprus;
there's a war on here! O please wake up.
Please be a dream. I've got to get back home!
Back to my cats. They'll starve. They'll eat the plants.
They'll be so lonely. *(to OTHELLO)* Please! I've got to go!
Where's the exit!?

OTHELLO   Stay!!!

CONSTANCE

Sure.

OTHELLO   Forty-thousand lives were not enough
to satisfy my debt to you, strange friend.
I'd keep you on this island till I knew
which angel beached you on our war-like shores,
and how you gained fair knowledge of foul deeds.

CONSTANCE

Well. Actually. I've studied you for years.

OTHELLO   You must be a learn'ed oracle.
I'd have you nightly search the firmament,
and daily read the guts of sheep for signs
to prophesy our battles with the Turk.

CONSTANCE

I only know of your domestic life.

OTHELLO   And of the murd'rous viper in my breast.
My shame is deeper than the Pontic sea,
which yet would drown in my remorseful tears,
whose crashing waves are mute before the trumpet cry
of this atoning heart would tumble Jericho!

CONSTANCE

Oh, well, I wouldn't dwell on it too much.
You'd never have been jealous on your own.

OTHELLO   O yes, I had forgot. *(to IAGO)* 'Twas all thy fault.
(to CONSTANCE) If that you be the mirror of my soul,
then you must learn the story of my life:
of moving accidents by flood and field,
of hairbreadth scapes i' th' imminent deadly breach,
of being taken by the insolent foe—

CONSTANCE

Oh yes, I know.

IAGO   *(aside)* So know we all the wag and swagger of this tale.

OTHELLO   In Egypt, kicked I sand into the eyes
of infidels who thought I made a truce

when I did give to them a pyramid
on wheels they pulled into the garrison.

But I had packed it full with Christian men,
who slit the savage throat of every Turk.

CONSTANCE

That sounds like Troy.

IAGO   *(aside)* Not Troy, but false.

CONSTANCE

And Desdemona fell in love with you,
because she loved to hear you talk of war.

OTHELLO   *These things to hear she seriously inclined.*

CONSTANCE

I've always thought she had a violent streak,
and that she lived vicariously through you,
but no one else sees eye to eye with me.
Yet I maintain, she did elope with you,
and sailed across a war zone just to live
in this armed camp, therefore—*(aside)* He's not a Moor.

IAGO   *(aside)* Amour? Ah-ha! *C'est ça! Et pourquoi pas?!*

A flourish of martial music.

OTHELLO   *Here comes the lady. Let her witness it.*

*Enter DESDEMONA attended by a SOLDIER who carries
her needlework.*

DESDEMONA

O valiant general and most bloody lord!

OTHELLO   *O my fair warrior!*

DESDEMONA

My dear Othello!

CONSTANCE

Divine Desdemona!

OTHELLO   My better self!

OTHELLO and DESDEMONA embrace.

IAGO   *(aside)* And my escap'ed prey. I'll trap thee yet.

DESDEMONA

> *That I love my lord to live with him,*
> *my downright violence and storm of fortunes*
> *may trumpet to the world. My sole regret—*
> that heaven had not made me such a man;
> but next in honour is to be his wife.
> And I love honour more than life! Who's this?

Everyone turns and stares at CONSTANCE.

CONSTANCE

> Hi… Desdemona…? This is like a dream….
>
> You're just as I imagined you to be.

> *CONSTANCE, in awe, reaches out to touch the hem*
> *of DESDEMONA's sleeve and fingers it throughout her*
> *next speech.*

> I'm Constance Ledbelly. I'm an academic.
> I come from Queen's. You're real. You're really real.

DESDEMONA

> As real as thou art, Constance, Queen of Academe.

CONSTANCE

> Is that my true identity? Gosh.
> I was just a teacher till today.

DESDEMONA

> A learned lady? O most rare in kind.
> And does your husband not misprize this knowledge?

CONSTANCE

> Oh, I'm not married.

IAGO   *(aside)* Most unnatural!

OTHELLO   A virgin oracle! Thanks be to Dian!

DESDEMONA

> Brave ag'ed maid, to wander all alone!

CONSTANCE

I'm really more of an armchair traveller.
In fact this is the biggest trip I've made.
I've only ever gone on package tours.

DESDEMONA

I long to hear the story of your life.

CONSTANCE

There isn't much to tell. It's very dull.
I'm certain your life's much, much more exciting.

DESDEMONA

This modesty becomes your royal self.
Othello, may she lodge with us awhile?

OTHELLO   I would she'd never leave these bristling banks.
She hath uncanny knowledge of our lives,
and sees us better than we see ourselves.
(to CONSTANCE) So now art thou my oracle and chaste.

OTHELLO grips CONSTANCE in a bear hug.

(to DESDEMONA) Hither sent by fortune, she hath saved me
from *perdition such as nothing else could match.*
Make her a darling like your precious eye.
(aside to CONSTANCE) You are her greatest friend.
But don't tell why.
(aside to IAGO) Deliver up the handkerchief, thou cur.

*OTHELLO takes the handkerchief and presents it
to DESDEMONA.*

IAGO   *(aside to OTHELLO)* I was just testing you, My Lord.

Exit OTHELLO and IAGO.

Michel Marc Bouchard (1958–)

LILIES

Translated by Linda Gaboriau

4M / 1F

Michel Marc Bouchard has written over fifteen plays, earning him many prizes in Quebec, across Canada, and worldwide over the last twenty years. *Lilies* was his first widely received drama and is now considered a major work of the Canadian theatre. It has won the Dora Mavor Moore Award and the Chalmers Canadian Play Award (1991), and has played in Ottawa, Montreal, Toronto, and internationally in France, Italy, Holland, and in South and Central America. Bouchard followed *Lilies* with other award-winning works, including *The Orphan Muses* (1994) and *Coronation Voyage* (1995). Like *Lilies*, both these plays have also been made into feature films.

A play within a play, *Lilies* is first set in Quebec in 1912 and then in 1952. It reveals a fifty-year conflict between the two main characters, Bishop Bilodeau and Simon Doucet. On the surface, the drama is the re-enactment of a murder acted out before Bishop Bilodeau by the inmates of a prison (not unlike Peter Weiss's asylum drama in *Marat/Sade*) directed by the protagonist Simon Doucet. As a teenager, Bilodeau, spurned by Simon as a lover in favour of Vallier, manipulates the illicit relationship by spreading malicious gossip and by finally killing Vallier, locking both he and Simon in a burning attic. After witnessing the re-enactment of his crime (for which Simon has spent his life in prison), the bishop recants his crime and begs Simon to kill him as a just punishment. The bitter prisoner refuses, leaving the bishop to the condemned life Simon, himself, has suffered.

Although Bouchard subtitles his play, "The Revival of a Romantic Drama," *Lilies* offers much more than love and courtly intrigue. First, the staging of Simon and Vallier's romance thematically pits the conservatism of the 1912 village of Roberval (and society in general) versus the rights of the individual, as the two adolescent homosexuals, Simon and Vallier, are beaten by family and persecuted by community. Secondly, Mme. Lydie-Anne and the countess, Vallier's mother, both provide imagination beyond romance. (Lydie arrives via an "aerostat," or balloon, from Paris, surely among the most exotic of stage entrances, while the countess believes she is a direct descendent of the

Bourbon Kings.) In Bouchard's own words, his characters often are "mistaken for my own inability to adapt to reality." *Lilies* engages both the intellect and the imagination.

In the following scene, the male prisoners re-enact the moment in 1912 when the seductive Lydie-Anne is first attracted to the beautiful, young Simon. She entices him into marriage and Simon agrees only to escape the persecution of Roberval. Worldly, witty, and attractive, Mademoiselle Lydie-Anne slyly enters this scene having overheard Simon describing to Baron de Hüe, a visiting doctor, the lashings he has received from his father for his homosexual behaviour. The scene ends with a young Bilodeau who is, himself, now smitten but rejected by the handsome Simon, sadistically enjoying his role as messenger for Lydie-Anne as she corners Simon into an unwanted marriage.

LYDIE-ANNE leaves her table.

LYDIE-ANNE

> *(to BARON DE HÜE)* May I? *(Without waiting for an answer, she sits down.)* This delightful breeze carries every sound, and I couldn't help but overhear your conversation. Allow me to say, young man, that you are a very bad liar, and it's a pity. With your looks you could be devastating.

BARON DE HÜE

> Madame!

LYDIE-ANNE

> *(to BARON DE HÜE)* He began by contradicting himself: "I already told you." "No, I forgot to tell you." A lie simply must begin with a positive sentence, not too emphatic, perhaps followed by a "Goodness, I forgot to tell you…" *(She laughs.)* It should put the person you're lying to in a position where he or she must participate in the lie: "Need I say?" Or be preceded by a compliment: "With your awareness of these things, you don't need me to tell you what you already know." And you carry on…. But you must avoid the kind of hesitation you just showed.

BARON DE HÜE

> Do you always take people for simpletons? Do you really think a doctor can't tell whether cuts are made by barbed wire?

LYDIE-ANNE

> I must point out that I was missing some of the details of the lie, but allow me to make up for it. Young man, why are you hiding the cause of your wounds?

SIMON

> *(angrily)* It's none of your business. *(suddenly sad)* It might spoil your lovely vacation, Madame!

LYDIE-ANNE

> *(gently)* You see that aerostat? It's mine. I got it in exchange for a few white lies. If I can ever be of any assistance… I would be delighted…

SIMON   Be careful, Madame. I might take you at your word.

> *They stare at each other. Long silence. VALLIER appears on the terrace.*

VALLIER   Simon!

LYDIE-ANNE
You are interrupting, young man.

VALLIER   Pardon me!

SIMON   What are you doing here?

VALLIER   An errand for my mother.

LYDIE-ANNE
Undoubtedly another patient for you, Doctor. Soon you'll need a nurse to assist you.

VALLIER   I went to see you, but your father told me that you were sick and couldn't have visitors. *(silence)* I thought that you'd at least come out to say goodbye to Father Saint-Michel. *(pause)* And what about the fire at the train station?

SIMON   *(indifferent)* I wasn't sick.

VALLIER   Timothée lied?

BARON DE HÜE
(sarcastically) Ah, it would seem that you have a disciple, Madame. I wonder what his approach is. He seems to have been convincing.

LYDIE-ANNE
You really don't want to understand my philosophy, do you? I landed in Roberval, expecting to meet a few Indians with war paint and feather headdresses. Just imagine my surprise when I met a real lady, not from the recent Napoleonic nobility, no, a true aristocrat, stranded in this...

VALLIER   You must be Mademoiselle de Rozier.

LYDIE-ANNE
That's the second time you've interrupted me, young man.

VALLIER   *(happy)* Pardon me. Please continue.

LYDIE-ANNE

She came up to me and asked whether I knew her husband, Count de Tilly.

SIMON So she got you too, eh? The minute a Frenchman arrives in Roberval, the countess pounces on him like a cat on a mouse, asking if he's seen her husband.

Hurt, VALLIER says nothing.

LYDIE-ANNE

The woman's situation is fascinating. Within five minutes I knew all her troubles. Her appearance betrayed her misfortune... her dress is several summers out of style. Her face is the face of someone who never has enough to eat. When she told me she has been hoping for some news from her husband for five years now, it was all I could do not to burst into tears.

SIMON You find that sad?

LYDIE-ANNE

I was devastated.

SIMON Well, people round here make fun of her. They think it's pretty funny, the way she takes her shack for a castle and thinks all the surrounding countryside belongs to her. The way she calls Lac Saint-Jean "the Mediterranean."

LYDIE-ANNE

So I talked to her about her husband. I pretended that I had met him in some of the most fashionable salons in Paris. I dug up gossip about a few old fallen barons and dead viscountesses forging some utopian revolution. You should have seen the look on her face, her smile, when I told her I had connections in Paris who could get news to her husband. I brightened up her day. Her son is supposed to bring me some letters.

VALLIER Here are my mother's letters, Mademoiselle de Rozier. I hope you'll have the decency to tear them up in front of me. You should be ashamed of lying to a poor woman...

LYDIE-ANNE

I should be ashamed? I made your mother happy, something which hadn't happened to her for five years. And I should be ashamed? Her happiness will last as long as this lie. Unless, of course, you insist upon distressing her... *(She tears up the letters.)*

VALLIER   I'd like to talk to you in private, Simon. *(He puts his hand on SIMON's shoulder.)* Simon?

SIMON   *(aggressively)* Get your hands off me!

BARON DE HÜE

Do you see where lying leads, Madame?

LYDIE-ANNE

You don't seem to understand, Doctor. These boys have a problem with the truth. Their eyes betray them. A pity that you work only on bodies. If you cared ever so slightly about the soul, you would see what I see.

BARON DE HÜE

You'll have to excuse me. I'm beginning to find the spring breeze tiresome. Simon, don't forget to tell your father I want to talk to him. *(He goes back into the hotel.)*

LYDIE-ANNE

I'll go along with you. I loathe moments of truth. Do wait for me, my friend. *(She catches up with BARON DE HÜE.)*

VALLIER   *(worried)* The whole village is over at the school. At the last minute, the principal assembled a choir to replace our play. We would have been performing *The Martyrdom of Saint Sebastian* at this very moment. The deputy arrived from Quebec City at noontime. The whole village turned out to greet him. And I stayed home with my mad mother. I was too unhappy. I missed you.

SIMON   *(mean)* So now you're gonna cry?

VALLIER   I don't understand why you ridiculed my mother.

SIMON	*(lifting his shirt to show his back to VALLIER)* Look at that, Vallier! You want to see my ass, too? See how it looks, thanks to your goddamn mother…
VALLIER	*(appalled)* Oh, my God! Did Timothée do that?
SIMON	That's right. My father did that to me. Thanks to your mother's blabbing about what I did to Bilodeau. I really liked the brave way you defended me. Shit, you could've made up something to confuse your mother. He was like a mad dog when he found me. He grabbed me by the arm and dragged me home. The minute we got inside the house, he went crazy. He pulled out all the dresses we kept after my mother died and he yelled: "Is this how you want to dress? Is that it?" He tied me to the bed while he drank his bottle of gin…. Then he took off his belt. "How many arrows did your goddamn saint get?" *(pause)* I passed out a couple of times, but he kept swingin' away till I got my twenty-two lashes. And he hit hard, really hard. Harder and harder. Again and again.
VALLIER	Oh, beloved. Oh, loved one!
SIMON	Lucky only the train station burned down, 'cause I finally got hold of myself. Shit! I could've set all of Roberval on fire.
VALLIER	I shall have Timothée punished.
SIMON	You're gettin' as crazy as your mother, Vallier. The only reason my father ever shows up at your place is that he keeps dreamin' some day you'll take him to Paris. Your mother hasn't paid him for three years. He even gives you all your firewood every winter, and whenever we have some supper left over, he takes it to you, like the other neighbours. "I shall have Timothée punished." You're as crazy as she is.
VALLIER	I forbid you to say that! She's not crazy. She's just playing her part. She's playing her part. She never could have survived the poverty and the isolation we've had to endure since my father left us, if she hadn't believed in her stories.
SIMON	You find that normal? You're gettin' as crazy as her, sayin' what you did to Bilodeau, about the two of us…

VALLIER   Simon, let's go down to the lake.

SIMON   Don't you understand? I don't want to have anything to do with you. It's all over. The attic, the hayloft, the closets, the lake! Don't you understand? Every time I go off with you, I'll be risking another beating. It's time for me to start thinkin' about girls.

VALLIER   I had a letter for you, too. I'd rather tear it up. *(He tears up the letter and puts it back into his pocket.)*

SIMON   Vallier, try to understand. I havta think about girls. Now don't start crying. I hate it when you cry.

   BILODEAU enters.

BILODEAU   Simon, Mademoiselle de Rozier wants to buy you a liqueur. And you, Lily-White, go play somewhere else. My father's the manager and he says this is no place for beggars.

   VALLIER leaves.

   (to SIMON as he passes him the drink) She'd like to talk you.

SIMON   Get lost, Bilodeau.

BILODEAU   I just wanted to do you a favour. When you're married to some nice, fat local girl and you havta spend your life shovelling sheep shit and cow manure to feed your fourteen kids, you'll remember the chance you had here on the terrace of the Hôtel Roberval. *(Pause. SIMON downs the cognac.)* Dontcha know how to say "Thanks"?

   LYDIE-ANNE enters.

LYDIE-ANNE
   Well, here I am, as arranged.

SIMON   What?

LYDIE-ANNE
   Didn't we agree that I would wait until you had finished your conversation before joining you?

SIMON   I never said that.

LYDIE-ANNE

And yet, I did wait. Whether it's true or false, I did wait.

SIMON So am I supposed to feel happy, like the countess?

LYDIE-ANNE

Now you're defending her?

SIMON I don't like goin' around talkin' about people.

LYDIE-ANNE

What I dislike most about this two-horse town is that no one ever says anything bad about anyone. Take that boy! *(pointing to BILODEAU)* He can't stop singing your praises.

SIMON You two make a fine pair of liars!

LYDIE-ANNE

People here are so good, so generous, and so absolutely kind.

SIMON We can't afford to spend all day gossiping. We got work to do, Madame.

LYDIE-ANNE

Except for you. You have the hands of a gentleman.

SIMON What does that mean?

LYDIE-ANNE

(takes his hands in hers gently) They're so soft and silky and white!

Judith Thompson (1954–)

PERFECT PIE

4F

Judith Thompson's plays have two things in common: they are driven by an emotional intensity and they win big awards. *White Biting Dog* (1984) and the anthology *The Other Side of the Dark* (1989) each won a Governor General's Literary Award, and *I Am Yours* (1987) and *Lion In The Streets* (1991) each won Chalmers Awards. In 2007 Thompson was awarded the fifty thousand dollar Walter Carson Prize by the Canada Council for her career in the Canadian theatre. She is arguably Canada's most accomplished playwright.

Although Thompson's plays have been called violent, bleak, and even brutal, in a very realistic way they open our eyes to the class prejudice and gender brutality of Canada's inner cities (*The Crackwalker, Lion in the Streets*) and its small towns (*Perfect Pie*). In the same way Canadian fiction writers like Alice Munro and Margaret Laurence portray the shadowy edges of their own small towns, Thompson's characters, the Patsy and Marie of *Perfect Pie*, illuminate the darkness at the end of their particular street.

Patsy, a housewife in the village of Marmora, Ontario, is visited by her childhood friend, Marie Begg, now a famous actress known as Francesca. The two women share a tragic secret from adolescence that has significantly altered both their lives. At the play's climax, they relive the night they both stood in front of an oncoming train in a suicidal pact to free themselves of the prejudice and violence of their small-minded town.

The play's tension is developed by the juxtaposition of scenes from the past with the present, over some thirty years. As Thompson steps the audience closer and closer to a full disclosure of Marie's teenage trauma, the adult Francesca and Patsy move backward in time toward a re-enactment of the same night.

These four consecutive scenes show the small-town religious and class prejudices that finally drive Marie away from Marmora and the warmth of a childhood friendship that has momentarily brought her back. The first begins with the two actors playing the young girls as Patsy rids Marie of head lice, making creative use of margarine. These are interposed with stories by the two older actors playing Patsy and Francesca as they share divergent views of men, marriage, and life.

Past.

First sleepover. PATSY is standing behind MARIE, picking nits. She wears gloves.

PATSY   Seventy-nine.

MARIE   Jeez.

PATSY wipes off her fingers.

PATSY   Eighty.

PATSY finds another.

MARIE   Holy crow. Don't tell nobody, eh?

PATSY   Eighty-one.

MARIE   My mother won't do this. She says no child of hers has lice.

PATSY   I don't mind doin' it. *I like it!* Eighty-two.

MARIE   Sometimes, at night? I'm lyin' in bed and the itchiness is so bad I think I'm just gonna jump out a window and run down the street screaming.

PATSY looks through her hair for more nits.

PATSY   And that's it for the nits. Looks pretty good. Yup. Now. Close your eyes real tight.

PATSY opens a tub of margarine.

MARIE   What are you going to do? What is that?

PATSY   Shhhh. It's margarine *(mar-ja-reen)*. It suffocates them.

MARIE   Wait. Wait. Aren't ya gonna get in trouble for takin' the margarine?

PATSY   Nope.

MARIE   Are you sure… this is what ya do?

PATSY   Yup.

MARIE	Is it going to feel yucky?
PATSY	No.
MARIE	Am I going to look stupid?
PATSY	No.
MARIE	How long will I have to have it for?
PATSY	Just till tomorrow. When we wake up. Then they'll all be dead. And then we comb 'em out.
MARIE	Oh, the smell!
PATSY	And you'll never have them again.
MARIE	Never?
PATSY	Never.
MARIE	Never.

***

Present.

PATSY continues making lunch. FRANCESCA is drinking her icewine.

PATSY	So. I've been dying to ask you. I hope you won't think I'm nosy. Those magazines say that you have been married three times. Now I know they are always tellin' terrible lies…
FRANCESCA	It's true!
PATSY	No way.
FRANCESCA	I know. It seems like a lot. But it just… happened that way.
PATSY	Round here nobody gets divorced even. Well, Sherry Bryden, she left Norm but he was beating on her and the kids, nobody thought the less of her. And come to think of it, the Andrews. Well let's just say its not common.

FRANCESCA

I thought each one was going to be forever. Except the third, which was just to help my friend Paulo get into the country.

PATSY Well now, that's interesting. That you thought they were going to be forever.

FRANCESCA

Hey, once a Catholic, always a Catholic. With the first, Douglas, we were so young. We had no money, we led this crazy downtown existence, living on mocha cake and jumbo martinis, running out of restaurants without paying, making terrible scenes in gay dance clubs, slapping people in the face, stealing lingerie from Holt Renfrew, and then being chased down Yonge Street by security, hiding in the bathroom of the Papaya Hut, gossiping viciously about everybody, passing rumours, destroying reputations. It was a lot of fun.

PATSY So what happened?

FRANCESCA

Oh, nothing. He turned out to be gay. I went back to school.

PATSY Gay?

FRANCESCA

Uh huh.

PATSY I don't think I've ever met anyone who's gay. I mean I've seen them, on television, and in movies.

FRANCESCA

Oh sure you have, Patsy.

PATSY Oh no, there's nobody gay in Marmora. I would know if there was.

Awkward moment. PATSY knows FRANCESCA thinks she is backward.

FRANCESCA

Well, people can be secretive, you know. When they know they will be… hated…. After all, no one wants to be another Marie Begg.

PATSY   Oh, you weren't hated.

FRANCESCA
Yes I was.

PATSY   I mean, it wasn't personal. You were just the scapegoat. Because
you were... arty.

FRANCESCA laughs.

Awkward pause.

I've often wondered, you know, if it still bothers you, ever,
when you think about it. Like, the way you were treated here,
as a kid.

FRANCESCA
Sometimes in a flash I am eleven years old again and they're
throwing stones at me. Calling me those names and coughing.
Remember? They used to cough when they saw me.

PATSY   Ignorant dogs.

FRANCESCA
On my bad days I think it was something in me. Something
they detected? Something that is... still there. You know?
There was a reason they picked on me, and not, say, Darlene
Rowan, who was also poor.

PATSY   Because Darlene, she knew her place, right? She never raised
her head!

FRANCESCA
So I walk out of my beautiful penthouse on the twentieth
floor feeling this big kind of dirty yellow stain all over me.
The Marie Begg Stain. I go to openings, dinner parties, book
launches, and I feel that people are avoiding the Stain. When
they do talk to me I can feel them wanting to get away from
the Stain. I see their eyes wandering and I feel the others are
whispering about me, all over the room, and then I think
I hear them coughing, they are coughing about me. And again,
I am the girl with the running sores and the scabby legs, the
lice and the dark circles under her eyes, and the crooked teeth.
I am Marie Begg. With the Stain.

PATSY   Well you look pretty clean to me, if it's any comfort.

FRANCESCA

You know, it's funny, I stand backstage sometimes and conjure... their faces and I am filled with a kind of electric energy, you know? And then I go out, like a lightning bolt; I guess it's revenge. I take my revenge on the stage somehow. *(pause)* Where are all those... people? Are they still... around?

***

Past.

MARIE has the rain bonnet on to keep the margarine in.

MARIE   Are you sure it's all right for me to sleep over?

PATSY   Yeah! You heard my mom.

MARIE   She is so nice. And so pretty. This is the first time I ever been on a sleepover.

PATSY   Really? How come?

MARIE   Because.

PATSY   I'm glad your mom said yes.

MARIE   I think she was drunk. Don't tell nobody I said that. What are we having for breakfast?

PATSY   French toast. With our own maple syrup.

MARIE makes the sign of the cross in gratefulness. PATSY notices.

Um, Marie? I have to ask you something. Are you... um... Catholic?

MARIE   What is French toast? Exactly.

PATSY   I like Catholics. It's okay.

MARIE   Like I know what French is. And I know what toast is.

PATSY   If you're Catholic, how come you don't go to St. Mike's?

MARIE   My mom said Father Duchene touched her titty.

PATSY	Shhhh.
MARIE	I mean… breast. Chest.
PATSY	My mom says to stay away from Catholic kids. She says they're tough. But I'll tell her you're nice…. I'll tell her you don't say bad words.
MARIE	I won't say no more.
PATSY	Thank you.
MARIE	That's why we don't have a farm anymore.
PATSY	Why?
MARIE	Because. We're Catholic.
PATSY	Oh. That's too bad.
MARIE	Because the Catholics got all the bad land. That's what my dad says. On the other side of the 401.
PATSY	So why don't you change to Protestant?
MARIE	I would but I can't, you know why? Because my gramma's last words, when she was dyin' on the bed and she held on to my hand so tight I couldn't let go? Her last words to me were, "Keep the faith." And that means "Stay Catholic." And then her eyes rolled up in her head.
PATSY	Ewww.
MARIE	I know.

***

Present.

PATSY	So number one was "that way." Who was the next husband?
FRANCESCA	
	Oh… Paul… handsome Paul…. I met him at McGill.
PATSY	So what happened?

FRANCESCA

We used to meet in his carrel, his study carrel? He was at the law school there. And the sex was indescribable. It even felt important, as if we were working for the French Resistance or something; he was by far the most passionate man I had ever met, but as soon as we got married, the DAY we got married, he started... to... raise his voice, no, yell at me.

PATSY   No way.

FRANCESCA

Just bellowed. All the time, about anything. A sock left on the floor. My dress being improper. My kissing, too hungry. And then one day, he threw a chair out the window.

PATSY   Oh my god. If there had been someone walkin' by with a baby in a stroller that chair coulda killed the baby.

FRANCESCA

That's exactly what I told him. And then I left. Didn't want my mother all over again.

PATSY   No, no ya wouldn't. *(pause)* What was he so damn mad about anyways?

PATSY finishes off her salad.

FRANCESCA

You really want to know? That time, specifically? I cut the banana cream pie with a spoon. He found that... careless.

PATSY   Hah! You used to do that around here, too!

FRANCESCA

I did?

PATSY   Yes! Oh my godfather, my mother would just shake her head.

FRANCESCA

I don't know why I did it. I just liked to use a spoon.

PATSY laughs. FRANCESCA laughs.

I just liked it!

They laugh harder. FRANCESCA helps with the placing of the cutlery.

I still do! But I realized something, you know. I realized that in that moment, he saw Marie. When I did that. Because that is something Marie would do. Not Francesca. And he certainly did not want to be married to Marie. Who would?

PATSY   Well I happen to like Marie, myself. I was disappointed when you threw away your name. Like you were throwin' my friend away, you know? I was disappointed… when you left. Did you know that?

FRANCESCA

…Lying in that hospital bed for all those weeks, with broken bones, I stared at the ceiling and I knew how I would end up if I stayed. I would end up the way they all thought of me because you can't keep fighting the way people think of you. Eventually, you have to give into it, and become it: I would be the strange schoolteacher living alone. Riding a bicycle with long hair and torn stockings, being called a witch by the schoolchildren; grandchildren of the people who had thrown rocks at me, and smeared dog shit all over my coat, and thrown my books all over the yard. And that's when I decided that I was going to leave, and leave Marie behind like the Thousand Island rat snake leaves behind his skin, and I was never, ever going to come back.

Timothy Findley (1930–2002)

ELIZABETH REX

4M /1F

As a young actor, Timothy Findley was a member of the original Stratford Festival company in 1950 with Alec Guinness. Later on, he began his more famous career as a playwright and author, highlighted by his third novel, *The Wars* (1977) and the premiere of *Elizabeth Rex* at Stratford in 2000. Both works received Governor General's Literary Awards.

Findley was an officer of the Order of Canada and honoured by the French government as a Chevalier de L'ordre des Arts et des Lettres, after spending many seasons at a second home in Cotignac in Provence. Over his career, he also received the Canadian Authors Association Award for Fiction, an ACTRA Award, the Order of Ontario, the Trillium Book Award, was a founding member and chair of the Writers' Union of Canada, and a president of the Canadian chapter of PEN International.

What follows is the final scene of the first act of Findley's brilliant conceit. Queen Elizabeth I has surprised Shakespeare's company of actors, the Lord Chamberlain's Men, by arriving in Stratford unannounced to spend the night of Shrove Tuesday, 1601, in the company of her favourite players.

According to Findley, his initial premise was to sketch the life of an older, Elizabethan actor who has made a successful career of playing female leading roles. The character of Ned Lowenscraft fits the bill. The company has just finished a performance of *Much Ado About Nothing*, which the queen tells Will she enjoyed, "in the extreme," especially Ned's role, the strong-minded Beatrice. But beyond these regal accolades, the audience learns Ned's career is doomed by advanced disease and Elizabeth is burdened by the fact she has sentenced her lover, Essex, to die at dawn the next day for treason. This scene is the first meeting between Ned and his queen and functions to show the similarity between these two very different lives. First, death looms large for each character; secondly, both Elizabeth and Ned have made careers of playing roles normally assigned to the opposite gender (hence the title); lastly, both have nothing to lose, and speak their minds openly. Thus, Queen Bess and Ned are as well matched as any Beatrice and Benedick.

Ned enters with his tame bear, unaware the queen has arrived in Shakespeare's Stratford barn. Elizabeth is attended by her young maid of honour, Lady Mary Stanley. The queen refers to Southampton, Shakespeare's patron, whom she has imprisoned with Essex, and to the handsome actor Jack Edmund who reminds the queen of Essex.

Mortality also plays two other roles in *Elizabeth Rex*. Although the play-length flashback is set in 1601, two years before Elizabeth's death, the initial scene of the play is set in April 1616, the night before Shakespeare's death. So, Shakespeare, Elizabeth, and Ned all face a final evaluation of their lives.

The distant music begins again—with a lighter touch.

ELIZABETH

Good. That's better music. Perhaps now that damned Irishman will return.

> *ELIZABETH holds out her tankard to STANLEY, who goes for ale. Meanwhile, NED enters up left, leading the bear by a chain. ELIZABETH does not see them.*

STANLEY　Madam…

ELIZABETH

(listening to the music) Be still.

STANLEY　But, Your Grace…

ELIZABETH

I have asked for *silence!!*

NED　*(a bit tipsy)* Who the rutting hell is that?

ELIZABETH

Silence!

NED　*(to the bear)* Luddy's brought in the fishmonger's daughter…

STANLEY　*Sir!!* How dare you!

NED　Oh, dear—a pair of 'em! Two bawds, *braying.*
He "brays," and then sings.
Two bawds went a-braying, O!
Two bawds went a-braying!
Two braying bawds for laying! O!
Two bawds went—

WILL　Ned. Tarry, sweet Beatrice.

> *NED turns, sees ELIZABETH, and falls down.*

NED　Dear Jesus Christ! Oh, dear Jesus Christ!

ELIZABETH

Why is the Lady Beatrice lying on her face?

The bear stands up and ambles down towards NED.

STANLEY   Oh—oh—Madam.

ELIZABETH
Has someone brought me a bear? Did I ask for a bear?

STANLEY   No, Madam.

ELIZABETH
Is he dangerous?

WILL   Not at all. He's quite well tamed.

ELIZABETH
Is he yours?

WILL   He belongs to Master Lowenscroft.

ELIZABETH
Beatrice has a bear! Wonderful! May one approach him?

WILL   Yes.

HARRY   Ned sleeps with him.

ELIZABETH
In a bed?

HARRY   Oh, yes. In the bear's arms. Here, they've been sleeping behind the bars in the granary—so's the bear won't frighten the horses—nor the dogs get near the bear.

ELIZABETH
Good bear. Sweet bear.

> *The bear stands and "speaks." ELIZABETH caresses his head.*

Master Lowenscroft, get up. I want an introduction to your bear. Has he a name?

NED   Harry.

ELIZABETH
I can't hear you.

WILL   Harry, Madam. He said *Harry.*

ELIZABETH

Shush. I want to hear it from him. From Beatrice.

WILL   Get up, Ned.

NED   Can't.

ELIZABETH

Rise!

NED rises.

And the dear bear's name?

NED   Harry. *(Mischief occurs to him. He smiles.)* Harry Wriothesley.

ELIZABETH

(to WILL) Your Harry, then. Southampton that is in the Tower with Essex.

NED   Some would have him brought from the Tower.

ELIZABETH

And some would not. He plotted against me.

NED   Not against the queen. Only for Lord Essex.

WILL   Ned...

ELIZABETH

And what has Southampton's name to do with bears?

NED   The bear was baited, Madam. Almost to death, by dogs. Everyone crying for his blood. I bought him from the keeper. Bears should go free.

ELIZABETH

You think Southampton is bear-like, Master Lowenscroft? Or merely baited.

NED   Baited.

ELIZABETH

By me? Or by circumstance...

NED   Circumstance didn't put him in the Tower.

ELIZABETH

The law towered him. The law... his peers.

NED

And if his peers had set him free, what would you have done then? Concur? Or sent them all to the Tower for their lack of judgment.

ELIZABETH

You have a great deal to say, for a woman.

NED

Yes. But I can shed *my* woman. *(He removes his cloak, revealing tights and a long white shirt.)* Here today—and gone tomorrow.

ELIZABETH

Your impertinence may be charming, Master Lowenscroft. It may also destroy you.

NED

I'm already destroyed.

ELIZABETH

Oh?

NED

The pox. As you can see...

ELIZABETH

We are all poxed, Master Lowenscroft—one way or another. Life is a pox. It leaves its scars on all of us.

NED

This pox kills, Madam.

ELIZABETH

Life kills. That is its purpose. Have you ever played the part of a queen, Master Lowenscroft?

NED

In *The Tragedy of King Richard the Third*, I played King Henry's widow.

ELIZABETH

Margaret, then.

NED

Yes.
Can curses pierce the clouds and enter heaven?
Why, then—give way dull clouds to my quick curses!
Long die thy happy days before thy death;
And after many lengthened hours of grief,
Die neither mother, wife, nor England's queen!

Absolute silence.

Unquote. *(He curtsies and rises.)* I also play Titania—*Queen of the Fairies!*

He "swishes" past ELIZABETH and drinks from his jar.

ELIZABETH

You have an extraordinary candour, Master Lowenscroft. Had you forgot I am your sovereign?

NED   No, Madam. I had forgot I was myself.

ELIZABETH

I admire your honesty. And, this night, I invite you to play whatever you choose. Whatever role—whatever temper. Will that fellow never come back?

WILL   Which fellow is that, Madam?

ELIZABETH

Your Benedick. I forget his name.

WILL   Edmund. Jonathan Edmund.

NED   Oh, he'll never come back. Not our Jack. He's in there bouncing all the ladies of the court.

ELIZABETH

Bouncing?

NED   Yes, Madam. Bouncing—trouncing—*pouncing!* With a hey, nonny-no—our Jack has gone a-bouncing-oh!

STANLEY   Master Lowenscroft.... The queen!

NED   The queen? Has the queen never bounced? *Bouncing— trouncing, and off with his head!* I thought that's what this was all about.

WILL   Ned.

ELIZABETH

Leave him. He proves an excellent sparring partner—not unlike your other fools.

NED   *Look, then to be well edified when the fool delivers the madman.*

WILL moves towards NED.

ELIZABETH
No, I say. Leave him. Let him be.

Commotion in the courtyard. Voices—dogs.

Vern Thiessen (1964–)

VIMY

4M / 1F

Choosing one short scene to represent Vern Thiessen's range as a playwright is not an easy task—there are too many compelling choices. Thiessen is also a fine example of how his generation of playwrights sees a broad, international perspective as unmistakably part of the Canadian canon.

Einstein's Gift is Thiessen's Governor General's Literary Award-winning drama on the life of Fritz Haber, the scientist in charge of Germany's chlorine gas attacks during the Great War. The playwright skilfully weaves the continual interlacing of science with warfare, especially in the twentieth century. Thiessen illustrates how even a pacifist like Albert Einstein, Haber's philosophical antagonist in the play, is ultimately drawn into its snare by his role in the atom bomb.

After the success of *Einstein's Gift*, Thiessen returned to the subject of World War I, only from an entirely different perspective. In *Vimy* (2007), the playwright draws six fictional characters before the backdrop of the Battle of Vimy Ridge—called by historians the symbolic birth of Canada as a nation. *Vimy* is a startling contrast to the grand figures and historical moments of *Einstein's Gift*. As Thiessen states in his introduction, it is an attempt "to discover how small actions can define us as individuals and as a nation."

In this scene from *Vimy*, Thiessen quickly escalates a typically Canadian argument over hockey to the level where the audience is forced to consider how conflict itself has defined our national character. It is our cultural diversity that ironically confirms our nationhood, as Nurse Clare reminds her charges in her "small action" that completes this scene.

The boys occupy themselves.

From away—the ever-present sounds of war.

CLARE enters, perhaps with linens.

J.P.   Any mail, miss?

CLARE   Nothin' but last month's newspaper.

             MIKE elects to take it.

             CLARE changes sheets.

J.P.   *Sacre*, when are we gonna get some mail!

CLARE   When it comes.

WILL   When can we go outside for a walk.

CLARE   When I tell you.

SID   I could really use a hot bath—

CLARE   Gentlemen! Please!

             From afar—shells.

MIKE   *(reading, then)* Can't be!

WILL   …What?

MIKE   *(reading)* You won't believe it.

J.P.   What are you mumbling about!

MIKE   *(reading)* "The Stanley Cup was awarded last month to…
             the Seattle Metropolitans"?!

             Outrage.

SID   What?!

J.P.   Get outta—!!

WILL   Seattle!?

MIKE	(*reading snippets*) "The first American team to win the Cup… faced the Montreal Canadiens, outscoring them nineteen to three."
J.P.	(*cursing*) *Batinse de cercueil!*
MIKE	"Frank Foyston, formerly of the Toronto Blueshirts, also scored heavily for Seattle."
J.P.	Foyston! (*spits*) Traitor.
WILL	An *American* team?
MIKE	Cyclone Taylor—now there's a player.
J.P.	Cyclone—? Anglo hack!
MIKE	Name me a better player, Frenchman!
J.P.	Newsey Lalonde!
MIKE	Newsey Lalonde!
J.P.	Best player ever lived.
MIKE	Nobody skates like Taylor!
J.P.	Nobody scores like Newsey!
WILL	Seattle? And we're fighting for this country *why*?
MIKE	Cyclone!
J.P.	Newsey!
SID	The Winnipeg Victorias won the Stanley Cup in—
J.P.	Winnipeg!?
MIKE	Beat Montreal!
J.P.	You don't know what you're talking about.
	From afar—a shell.
CLARE	Hockey was invented in Nova Scotia.
J.P.	First game with rules, Quebec!
WILL	Kingston, it was King—!
SID	The Irish brought it over—!

MIKE	It was INDIANS first played it.
J.P.	Is that so?
MIKE	Lacrosse on ice.
J.P.	You Indians gotta do everything first, huh?
MIKE	Been in the country a helluva lot longer than the French.
J.P.	Not our fault you gave it away.
MIKE	Gave it—?!

A shell—closer.

CLARE	Boys…
J.P.	Why you fighting anyway.
MIKE	Why?!
J.P.	What do you care?
MIKE	Helluva lotta Indians signed up for this war. We got whole reservations don't have a man over eighteen on 'em. Now you tell me, Frenchie, how many of your guys signed up?
J.P.	My friend Claude and me, that's who!
WILL	Hey, hey—
SID	Come on guys—
MIKE	*(to J.P.)* All you care about is getting your walking papers.
J.P.	So what if I do?
MIKE	Guys are dying out there—
J.P.	And I'm gonna go home and tell them what a crazy, stupid war this really is.
SID	All right, all right—
WILL	That's enough—
MIKE	You think a little shell shock's gonna get you home, Frenchie?
J.P.	Shut up, ya red-skinned—
MIKE	'Cause you'll be the FIRST to get sent back to the line, ya COWARD!

SID   Whoa!

WILL   Come on now!

J.P.   Ferme ta gueule, stupide, salot, enfant de chienne de bâtard...!
            [Shut your mouth, you dirty, stupid, son-of-a...!]

>   *J.P. and MIKE go after each other.*

>   *Yelling.*

>   *Finally:*

CLARE   Stop it!
            Stop It!
            STOP IT!!!

>   *They separate.*

What is WRONG with you!?
You think I came here for this?
You think I left my, my *life*... for THIS?

>   *They are silent.*

(firm) You think you're the only ones want to go home? You think you're the only ones want to do good? You think you're the only ones hurtin'? You think you're the only ones who gave up something?

Well you're not. I see dozens of ya every single day. Every DAY. And for every one of you, there's another hundred out there.

So you tell me: why should I bother? Why should I bother putting you back together, if all you're going to do is tear each other apart? You tell me.

(a real question) TELL ME!

>   *Another shell, lingering, like a memory.*

>   *They are silent.*

>   *She moves away.*

Catherine Banks (1957–)

BONE CAGE

2M / 2F

Catherine Banks began her writing career while raising her two children and working as an educator in Nova Scotia. Her works include *Eula's Offer*, *The Summer of the Piping Plover*, *Bitter Rose*, and *Three Storey Ocean View*, her most awarded work until the GG for *Bone Cage* in 2008. Since then, Banks has written two new plays, *Missy and Me* and *It is Solved By Walking*.

It is very difficult to find one scene that adequately reflects her honest portrayal of characters and their profound frustrations, that illuminates the poetry of Banks's dialogue and its complex imagery, and that shows the wonderful turns of plot and brilliant theatricality of *Bone Cage*. It is a play that is admired best in its entirety. Like celebrated Canadian novelist, David Adams Richards, Catherine Banks portrays youth marginalized by a resource economy, whose lack of education and opportunity cages their ambitions and eats at them from within.

Chicky, her half-brother Jamie, his bride Krista, and her teenage brother Kevin all live in a small, Nova Scotia village in the heart of pulp country, where the trees beyond the visible corridor of the highway have all been ravaged by a lumber industry rapidly running out of resources. Jamie hates his job on the tree processor, a bush machine so destructive it leaves a trail of dead wildlife in its wake. To regain some humanity, he salvages wounded birds and their eggs after a day's work. Banks uses this event to begin her extended imagery of the nest, the cage, and hearts limited by circumstance. Further expanding the imagery with her name is Chicky, who works a cutter on a sod farm, and feels, like Jamie, "used up and spit out" by her work—a metaphor for the destructive machinery they drive. In her case, she is also used by Reg, an older, married man who she sees for no other reason than he took her virginity at fifteen. Krista, seventeen, and the only character whose dreams are still largely unspoiled (although Jamie and Chicky try their best) is preoccupied with her upcoming wedding to Jamie. Kevin, her eighteen-year-old brother who works chainsaw alongside Jamie, is preoccupied with sex—particularly with Chicky—although he has recently been sexually abused by Merv, the town bully. (Later, we learn Chicky has good reason to keep her distance—both she and Kevin share the same parent.) Clarence, Jamie and Chicky's disabled father, has his own destructive obsession—he intends a bizarre cloning (through a DNA sample from the gravesite) of his first son, Travis, the child who died years before and on whom he pinned his dreams, much to Jamie's disgust.

Thursday morning. KRISTA sits at the table writing out thank you notes. JAMIE comes in carrying a beer and three partridge eggs.

KRISTA   Ten more for you to sign.
I'm not bringing them shower gifts into this house.
I'll keep them at home till we move to the trailer.
Same with the wedding ones, too.

       JAMIE puts the eggs on the table. She touches the eggs.

They're cold.
What's a hen suppose to do with partridge babies anyway?
You shouldn't do that. Walk around looking for them after your shift.

JAMIE   You hear them when you get out of the machine.

KRISTA   You can't hear eggs.

JAMIE   Jesus, I hear their mothers looking for their nests, looking for their babies.

KRISTA   I know you can't hear eggs. I was kidding, Fuzzy.

JAMIE   I told you, don't call me that.

KRISTA   Chicky does. The men at the fire hall all do.

JAMIE   I don't want you to.

KRISTA   That's not fair.

JAMIE   Come here.

      JAMIE kisses her and whispers something in her ear. She looks at him.

KRISTA   What do you mean?

JAMIE   Mom said "Jamieeee" like "what are you up to, you little shit."
Clarence says Jamie like "not Travis," the one he wants alive.
Like "*Not Travis*, you going to the liquor store today?"

> *KRISTA crawls onto his lap. Kisses him on the mouth.*

And when the teachers said "Jamie," well, weren't they thinking dumb-ass?

KRISTA   Jamie, stop—

JAMIE   There.

KRISTA   What?

JAMIE   Even when you are pissed at me. There's something—you say Jamie like there's a chance of something… in me.

KRISTA   Jamie jamie jamie jamie jamie…

> *They kiss.*

Want to?

JAMIE   I'm saving myself till I'm married.
I can wait.

> *KRISTA kisses him.*

I might have to take a trip to the vet before supper.

The eagle's not looking too good.
He's losing feathers. His eyes look milky.

KRISTA   Half what you rescue dies.
Like that baby racoon that time.
Like those eggs.
Is that why you're quitting? Chicky told me.

> *JAMIE speaks his line to the bedroom door, indicating that he knows she is in there.*

JAMIE   Sis needs to keep her nose out of my business.

KRISTA   It's my business. I'm marrying you the day after tomorrow.

JAMIE   I don't work chainsaw.

KRISTA   That don't make sense. You hate what the processor does, but you won't work chainsaw. You got to have a job.

JAMIE	That's the thing, Krista, in ten years there won't be logging jobs around here. The woods is tapped out. In ten years, *less even*, there won't be any trees in this valley.
KRISTA	What are you talking about? It's woods all the way to town and that's over forty miles.
JAMIE	You don't know what you're looking at. All along the roads is not woods anymore. What you're seeing is a screen of trees, two, three tier deep, and behind that hectares and hectares of clear-cut.
	Everything has been chewed up and spit out. Not one tree standing.
	That's why…. Listen, Krista, I'm not saying we can afford to do this right away but I'm thinking—
	KEVIN bursts in.
KEVIN	Where's Clarence?
JAMIE	Jesus, Kevin, what's crawled up your ass?
KEVIN	Is he here? Where is he?
	CHICKY comes out of the bedroom.
	Chicky, where's Clarence?
CHICKY	It's the colostomy clinic day at the hospital.
JAMIE	The fun never stops for old Clarence.
KEVIN	Good, good, 'cause if he hears this, he's gonna have a stroke or something.
CHICKY	Kevin, what are you talking about?
KEVIN	They're burying Betty's boy tomorrow, right?
CHICKY	I told him not to call Betty again. He's telling them to send the body to Florida to be frozen.
KEVIN	No, Chicky, Ronnie went over to check the gravesite and he saw. They've been fucking with Trav's grave.
CHICKY	Who has?

JAMIE	What did you have to tell her for, Kev? Jesus.
CHICKY	Fuzzy, what's he talking about?
JAMIE	It's okay, Chicky. I've taken care of it. I'm getting sod from Reg.
CHICKY	Sod, for what?
JAMIE	It was probably some animal digging around. Forget it.
KEVIN	Ronnie says it weren't no animal. They like dug a big hole straight down the middle of the plot—got Betty all upset. Fucking Merv.
CHICKY	Why would he bother Trav's grave?
KEVIN	*Someone* laid a beating onto him at Jamie's stag so he's paying him back.
CHICKY	*Jamie.*
JAMIE	Do you see a mark on me?
KEVIN	Don't blame Jamie, we was only getting back at Merv for what he did to me.
CHICKY	This has gone far enough, Kevin. Merv's got kids.
KEVIN	He don't act like it. If you got kids you don't dig up some other kid's grave.
JAMIE	No—not some other kid's grave. Kev. Go get the sod from Reg, okay?
KEVIN	What about Merv?
CHICKY	You don't know that it was him.
KEVIN	You kidding? You tell her, Jamie.
JAMIE	Maybe it wasn't.
KEVIN	Jamie, he did it, I know it, you know it.
JAMIE	I'll meet you at the grave—make it look like nothing happened there for Betty tomorrow.
KEVIN	Let me, Jamie. I'll fix it up right.

> Then I'm going to go get that son of a bitch.

> *KEVIN leaves. CHICKY looks at KRISTA.*

CHICKY Are you going to do something?

KRISTA What? Besides Merv... he started it, right?
Kevin will be a mess in the wedding photos.

CHICKY I don't care about your *(fucking)* wedding pictures.

KRISTA See, Jamie? Make her stop ruining our wedding.
Well?
I'm going home.

> *KRISTA seems to expect JAMIE to go with her.*

> I said I'm going home.

> *KRISTA leaves, clearly angry.*

CHICKY I don't think even Merv would do something like that.

JAMIE It don't matter to Kevin who did it.
He needs for it to be Merv.

CHICKY Why?

JAMIE Look, Chicky. Merv did something to Kev, Kev's got to take
Merv on. If he wants to live around here anyways.

CHICKY What did he do to Kev to make him so crazy?

JAMIE I don't ask what Merv the perv does. You saw him. They got
him good and drunk, that's for sure. Maybe they fed him some
Viagra, made him look at someone's dick and told him if his
pecker got hard it meant he's a queer. Anyway, you know they
got his underwear off him one way or another.

CHICKY He's acting like he's going to kill Merv.

JAMIE If Kevin got laid, sis, he'd be all right.

CHICKY You know, he might be the same to me as you.

JAMIE You're putting a lot of faith in shit Mom told you.

CHICKY You tell Kev, that's enough.

JAMIE	I'll tell, don't mean he'll listen.
CHICKY	When are you going to BC?
JAMIE	Soon enough.
CHICKY	Not soon enough. You've had that ad for months. Have you called?
JAMIE	That ain't your business, but yes, I did.
CHICKY	So you are going?
JAMIE	Soon as I get the money together.
CHICKY	You *quit* your job.
JAMIE	Danny's renting the trailer till spring. We'll have enough to move out there by then.
CHICKY	You might have the wedding paid off by then. Why are you marrying her? It's not like you're lovesick.
JAMIE	Now you sound like her. "Do you love me? Do you really, really love me?" Fuuuuuuuuuuuuuuuuuuuccccccccccckkkkkkkk.
CHICKY	She'll stop you from going.
JAMIE	No she won't. Krista's going too.
CHICKY	You'd do better on your own.
JAMIE	I need one person with me who knows me.
CHICKY	You marry her, you'll be stuck. She'll get pregnant…
JAMIE	No, we ain't having kids for a long time.
CHICKY	You're being a stupid married man, and you're not even married.
JAMIE	Yeah, I heard Carol's preggers.
CHICKY	Yeah, well, so I know what I'm talking about.
JAMIE	You know, sis, old Reggie's using you up, same as he's using up the interval land. What are *you* sticking around for?

CHICKY	Haven't you noticed I've been taking care of you?
JAMIE	So now you don't have to. And don't wait around here for some someday family reunion. Mom probably doesn't know who your father is, for sure.
CHICKY	I can't stand living with you sometimes.
JAMIE	I'm not saying anything against you. It's her I'm talking about.
CHICKY	You used to have a heart. You used to have feelings.
JAMIE	Yeah?
CHICKY	You weren't like this before.
JAMIE	Before when?
CHICKY	I don't know. Before Travis died. Before you quit school. Before you started drinking every day.
JAMIE	You know what I feel these days?
CHICKY	What?
JAMIE	*(pause)* Nothing.
CHICKY	No… tell me.
JAMIE	Nothing is what I feel after a twelve-hour night shift shaking inside that machine. Hearing everything outside it get tore up. The men say don't walk around a section you've just clear-cut. Earl and them say if it makes you feel bad don't do it. I can't just walk away… leave things half-dead and dying.
CHICKY	Is that why you're drinking, causing trouble with Merv?
JAMIE	Merv isn't anything. All that is just… something stupid to do. What makes you feel better after a sunny afternoon of stripping the topsoil off interval land?
CHICKY	I certainly don't go beating up people.
JAMIE	Have you looked at Reg's wife lately? Carol looks like you've given her a bruising more than once.
CHICKY	Jesus.
JAMIE	And you're worried about what I'm doing to Merv's kids?

CHICKY Jesus, you've got some nerve.
Well, I'm not being the maid of honour for your funeral.

JAMIE I told her you will.

CHICKY walks out the door.

You are right, sis, I have some nerve, but it's shot to hell.
Nothing another beer won't fix.

JAMIE takes a long drink.

Lights out.

PART FOUR

Scenes for More

Kent Stetson (1948–)

THE HARPS OF GOD

10 M

Kent Stetson seems to possess the rare ability to join the past with the present, the local with the universal, the authentic with the poetic. The powerful characterizations in Stetson's epic about the 1914 seal hunt disaster, *The Harps of God*, strikes this fine balance, as do his first plays, *Warm Wind in China* (Neptune Theatre, 1988) and *Queen of the Cadillac* (Alberta Theatre Projects, 1990), and the more recent *Horse High, Bull Strong, Pit Tight* (Theatre Prince Edward Island, 2001) and *New Acadia*, for which won the 2001 Herman Voaden National Playwriting Competition. Many of his plays have been quickly adapted for film; no surprise given their visual appeal generated from Stetson's talent as a scriptwriter.

In addition to the 2001 GG for *The Harps of God*, Stetson's work has won the Carol Bolt Award (2002), and PEI's Wendell Boyle (2002) and Literary Arts (2007) awards. Stetson also enjoys a career as a dramaturge, teaching the craft of playwriting both formally (at the National Theatre School and McGill and Concordia universities) and through his website, www.masterplayworks.com.

The GG jury citation applauded Stetson's creation of a new theatrical language—"both authentic to the Newfoundland idiom and as powerful and economic as poetry… The play explores faith and meaning and pays tribute to the survival of a people and a nation." Stetson has directed some of his own works and plays by Berni Stapleton and Don Druick. In 2007 Kent Stetson was appointed to the Order of Canada. In the same year, he received the Prince Edward Island Council of the Arts and the PEI Writer's Federation Award for Distinguished Contribution to the Literary Arts On Prince Edward Island. Stetson is based in Montreal, but works extensively in PEI.

The Harps of God recounts the tragic seal hunt of 1914 when one hundred thirty-two men were abandoned by their ships for two days and nights on the ice floes of the North Atlantic.

Two-thirds of them did not survive. Stetson's play puts the audience on the ice with the sealers, first as they go about their grim livelihood, then as they slowly realize they are not going to survive. This scene, from early in the play, reveals the conflicts among the men and their view of the work they must do to earn a living.

LEVI   Make two small slits just above the h'eye.
Pass your 'aul rope t'rough.

DAWSON   Here ye go, Billy.

>   *Club.*

I'll kill em, you sculp 'em, till ye gets the hang of it.

BILLY   Them big black eyes lookin' at me.
What am I to think?

MULLOWNEY
I thinks of me youngsters,
All decked out in new shoes and coats.
Then *Whammo!*

>   *Club.*

One less seal, that many more cod fish,
The youngsters turned out proper;
The pride of Pouch Cove.

MCCARTHY
(club) The merchant off of me back for half an hour.

DAWSON   Think of yer old retriever, Billy,
The day we put him out of his misery.
What a wonderful relief it was to the lot of us.

BILLY   Includin' the dog?

MULLOWNEY
I thinks of Mamie's big pink thighs,
On a blowy Saturday night.

LEVI   There's no call for yer dirty Irish smut, Mullowney.

MULLOWNEY
Mind yer business, you arse-clenched Protestant killjoy.
Mamie and me dancin' and dancin' and...
Oh, Jesus boys.

    Club.

    I miss me Mamie somethin' fierce.

DAWSON   Hop to it, Billy.

    Club.

    Ye're one behind already.

LEVI   Captain Kean says this year'll provide the biggest bill ever, Despite the late start.

JORDAN   Another Eldorado spring.

SIMON   Rumours of war in Europe 'ave sent the price of seal oil skyrocketin'.

ANDREW   There's all kinds of uses for the fat—

SIMON   Oil for the soldiers' guns—

ANDREW   Oil for the machines that'll stitch their uniforms.

JORDAN   Fine, light oil, seal oil.

MCCARTHY

    What soldiers?

ANDREW   We're goin' to make our fortune, Billy.

MULLOWNEY

    There's talk of war in Europe; where ye been, b'y?

MCCARTHY

    Home, me son.

    Club.

    Mindin' me own business.

JORDAN   Them boys of yer's 'ave got right knowin'.

LEVI   I took 'em to the Nickel in St. John's town.

JORDAN   The things youngsters learns at them damn movin' pictures.

LEVI   *(club)* Shockin'.

BILLY   Where's their harps to?

ANDREW   It's only the growed-up cows and dogs got the harp.
Eh, father?

LEVI   That's right, me son.
And why's that, do ye suppose?

ANDREW   *(sculping)* When God hurled Lucifer into the abysmal deep,
There was a great racket and row in heaven.
God's favourite possession—
A little harp, made of solid gold,
Wit' the sweetest voice ever heard—
Was knocked off of her cloud and plummeted into the ocean.

LEVI   God was fit to be tied.

   Club.

   Why? Simon!

SIMON   First he's forced to throw Our Saviour's big brother Satan
out of 'eaven.
Then he loses his most cherished possession.

LEVI   Satan was the older brother of God, not Jesus.
God was about to loose his mighty vengeance upon the earth…
What 'appened? Andrew!

ANDREW   He heard the sweetest of sounds.
Yes, sir. He did. Down north—off of the Labrador—
Glintin' like a miracle above the tempest tossed sea…
There she was, b'ys;
The little gold 'arp of God.

BILLY   No!

LEVI   Yes. Simon!

SIMON   Yes, father.
A young dog seal—a beater, not yet a bedlamer,
Just after losin' his white coat and takin' to the water—
Seen the glitterin' object waft downwards to the floor of the sea.
Now, seals is a wonderful, playful creature, as we all knows.
That's why they gets so tangled in our nets,
Rippin' and tearin', causin' no end of labour.
Ruinin' our hard work.

Club.

Damn their hides.

LEVI   Bless their 'ides fer the life they gives, says I. Andrew!

ANDREW   This young seal seen there was somethin' particular about the
golden 'arp.
Not only did she hum the loveliest tune,
But she spoke to the young beater and said—

BILLY   No, Skipper Levi b'y! She never! She spoke?

LEVI   Oh, yes my son. She said…
"Take me home to me fadder, and 'e will reward ye."
Well sir. He took her in his mouth,
Swam to the surface and danced in the wind and foamin' waves,
Balancin' God's 'arp on his nose, safe among the starm.
The wind caused her strings to quiver, then 'um—
Then, Oh…!
That mournful song.
My son.
God was that pleased.
You know what he done?

Club.

He took back his harp and said to the beater—Simon!

SIMON   Yes, father.
God says to the young swile:
"Thank you, my son.
As a sign of my pleasure, you will bear the shape of my 'arp
on yer back.
Yer children will sing her mournful song.
For yer supper, I'll make the seas team wit' fishes like nowhere
else on earth.
I'll cause ye and yer tribe to swell in yer multitudes till the end
of time."

Art MOULAND enters. JESSOP Templeman follows.

LEVI   Andrew!

ANDREW   The beater said "Thank ye, heavenly father."
For as we knows, swiles could talk back then—

MCCARTHY

That's right.

Club.

And tight-arsed moralizin' old Protestants wasn't invented yet.

ANDREW   "But we am perfectly happy the way we is,"
Says he, and swum away.

LEVI   God was beside himself wit' rage:
"Why you uppity little bag of fat and guts.

Club.

Thinks your perfect, does ye?
I'll have none of that."
God was that angry. Why? Simon!

MOULAND   Go ahead, Jessop.

JESSOP   Father, I come to say—

LEVI   Simon.

JESSOP   I come to say I'm sor—

LEVI   Simon!

SIMON   Because from the moment of creation until then,
The souls of all God's creatures—men, seals, fish, everyt'ing—
Was in perfect 'armony wit' his own.
Perfect as the sounds from the 'arp of God.

LEVI   That's right.
Every thing and everybody knowed their place in the scheme
of things.
God in 'eaven at the top, the lowest worm on the bottom;
Mankind in between.
And God gave man dominion over everyt'ing that walked,
Squawked, crawled on its belly, flew in the air or swum in
the sea.

MCCARTHY
Then, for some damn reason,

Club.

He invented merchants.

LEVI   That trouble wit' Lucifer broke out.
All hands started singin' their own tune.
We all knows where that leads to.
God called him back.
"In yer arrogance you deny me;
From this day forward, you will offer your very skins
And those of your children,
To the sons of men for their benefit;

Club.

At my pleasure." Andrew!

ANDREW   Yes, father. Mr. Swile dove, rose up,
Broke the surface wit' a wonderful flip, and said:
"They'll have to catch me first."

LEVI   So God took the swile's arrogant, willful voice from him;
Made 'im croak like a frog; bark like a dog.
Then 'e hobbled the disobedient creature's youngsters.
Made them creep about on the oice on their bellies,

Club.

Easy pickin's
For the great ice bear and the sons of men.

MULLOWNEY
Fairy stories.
Sure, the truth of the matter is we'm hungry and them is food.
Food and clothes for me.

Club.

And my Mamie.

Wajdi Mouawad (1968–)

SCORCHED

Translated by Linda Gaboriau

3M / 5F

Born in Lebanon, Wajdi Mouawad came to Canada in 1977 at the age of nine. Like many other successful Canadian playwrights of his generation, Mouawad attended Montreal's National Theatre School and then worked as an actor, director, and writer. In 1999, he was named artistic director of Theatre Quat'Sous; in 2007, he assumed a similar position for a five-year term with the National Arts Centre's French Theatre in Ottawa.

Scorched is Mouawad's second play in a proposed tetralogy. The first play of this ambitious series was Littoral (in English, Tideline) which won the Governor General's Literary Award for Drama in French in 2000. Both plays (and presumably, the tetralogy) are concerned with themes of the immigrant experience, in particular, memories of a war-torn homeland and its violent imposition on the family. Tideline explores the barely imaginable difficulty of burying a parent who, as a result of war, is essentially without a homeland, or a place to be buried in peace. Similarly, Scorched deals with what a Canadian brother and sister learn about their mother and thus their earlier lives when faced with her burial.

Two other defining elements that distinguish both plays from many contemporary dramas are Mouawad's deliberate use of a collaborative writing process and the expressionistic style of his language. In his introduction to Scorched (Incendies in French) the playwright explains that the collaborative development process is at the heart of his playwriting technique:

> Like Littoral, Incendies never would have seen the light of day without the participation of the actors.... The actors were revealed through the characters and the characters were revealed through the actors.... Throughout the entire period, I felt that the troupe, with its technicians and actors laying the groundwork for the writing, was at the heart of the process.... It must be said, it must be heard: Incendies was born of this group, the writing was channelled through me. Step by step to the very last word.

One cannot help but recall the groundbreaking Canadian collective creation, *The Farm Show*. Under the direction of Paul Thompson, it grew in a similar fashion—from the input of the actors. As Ted Johns, a major collaborator of the scripted version, wrote in his introduction, "The dramatic techniques, and the songs grew out of the actors' attempts to dramatize their discoveries in daily improvisational sessions."

Thus, this excerpt was chosen first to illustrate this historical connection. The collective creation characteristically employs short scenes and the unexpected juxtaposition of one place and/or time against another. In *Scorched*, Mouawad's semi-comic figure of Lebel, the Montreal lawyer, establishes the present: Nawal's death and the administration of her will by her son and daughter. Lebel's odd demand for buckets of water at the Montreal graveside makes perfect sense to an audience who has witnessed the previous scene, set years before and miles away. The unlikely use of the clown's nose in scene eight draws a similar creative juxtaposition that echoes throughout the play. These are elements born of improvisation, generated through collective creation and characteristic of Mouawad's plays.

Secondly, Mouawad's two most well-known dramas are both notable in their use of expressionism, especially in the set and language of *Scorched*. The set of "white trees" referred to in scenes five and seven (which visually dominate the stage throughout the production) and the language, particularly Nawal's long monologue in scene five and Wahab's in scene seven, are both strongly reminiscent of two much earlier pioneers of Canadian theatre: the sets of Herman Voaden (in *Hill-Land*, for example) and the language of Gwen Pharis Ringwood in *Drum Song*. (Ringwood, too, attempted to model elements of classical tragedy to strengthen her dramas which, Mouawad explains in his introduction to *Tideline*, he has attempted as well.) In Wajdi Mouawad's plays, there are strands of a Canadian tradition.

Dawn. A forest. A rock. White trees. NAWAL (age fourteen).
WAHAB.

NAWAL   Wahab! Listen to me. Don't say a word. No. Don't speak. If you say a word, a single word, you could kill me. You don't yet know the happiness that will be our downfall. Wahab, I feel like the minute I release the words about to come out of my mouth, you will die too. I'll stop talking, Wahab, so promise me you won't say anything, please, I'm tired, please, accept silence. Shhhh! Don't say anything. Don't say anything.

She falls silent.

I called for you all night. I ran all night. I knew I'd find you at the rock where the white trees stand. I'm going to tell you. I wanted to shout it so the whole village would hear, so the trees would hear, so the night and the moon and the stars would hear. But I couldn't. I have to whisper it in your ear, Wahab, and afterwards I won't dare hold you in my arms, even if that's what I want most in the world, even if I'm sure I'll never feel complete if you remain outside me, and even if I was just a girl when I found you, and with you I finally fell into the arms of my real life, I'll never be able to ask anything of you again.

He kisses her.

I have a baby in my belly, Wahab! My belly is full of you. Isn't it amazing? It's magnificent and horrible, isn't it? It's an abyss, and it's like freedom to wild birds, isn't it? And there are no more words. Just the wind! I have a child in my belly. When I heard old Elhame tell me, an ocean exploded in my head. Seared.

WAHAB   Maybe Elhame is wrong.

NAWAL   Elhame is never wrong. I asked her, "Elhame, are you sure?" She laughed. She stroked my cheek. She told me she's the one who has delivered all the babies in the village for the last forty years. She took me out of my mother's belly and she took my mother out of her mother's belly. Elhame is never wrong. She promised she wouldn't tell anyone. "It's none of my business," she said, "but in two weeks at the most, you won't be able to hide it anymore."

WAHAB   We won't hide it.

NAWAL   They'll kill us. You first.

WAHAB   We'll explain to them.

NAWAL   Do you think that they'll listen to us? That they'll hear us?

WAHAB   What are you afraid of, Nawal?

NAWAL   Aren't you afraid? *(beat)* Put your hand here. What is it? I don't know if it's anger, I don't know if it's fear, I don't know if it's happiness. Where will we be, you and me, in fifty years?

WAHAB   Listen to me, Nawal. This night is a gift. It might be crazy for me to say that, but I have a heart and it is strong. It is patient. They will scream, and we will let them scream. They will curse and we will let them curse. It doesn't matter. After all that, after their screams and curses, you and I will remain, you and I and our child, yours and mine. Your face and my face in the same face. I feel like laughing. They will beat me, but I will always have a child in the back of my mind.

NAWAL   Now that we're together, everything feels better.

WAHAB   We will always be together. Go home, Nawal. Wait till they wake up. When they see you, at dawn, sitting there waiting for them, they will listen to you because they will sense that something important has happened. If you feel scared, remember that at that very moment, I'll be at my house, waiting for everyone to wake up. And I'll tell them, too. Dawn isn't very far away. Think of me like I'll think of you, and don't get lost in the fog. Don't forget: now that we're together, everything feels better.

        WAHAB leaves.

                        ***

In NAWAL's house.

Mother and daughter (age fourteen).

JIHANE	This child has nothing to do with you, Nawal.
NAWAL	It's in my belly.
JIHANE	Forget your belly! This child has nothing to do with you. Nothing to do with your family. Nothing to do with your mother, nothing to do with your life.
NAWAL	I put my hand here and I can see his face.
JIHANE	It doesn't matter what you see. This child has nothing to do with you. It doesn't exist. It isn't there.
NAWAL	Elhame told me. She said: "You are expecting a baby."
JIHANE	Elhame isn't your mother.
NAWAL	She told me.
JIHANE	It doesn't matter what Elhame told you. This child does not exist.
NAWAL	And when it arrives?
JIHANE	It still won't exist.
NAWAL	I don't understand.
JIHANE	Dry your tears!
NAWAL	You're the one who's crying.
JIHANE	I'm not the one who's crying, your whole life is pouring down your cheeks! You've gone too far, Nawal, you've come back with your spoiled belly, and you stand here before me, in your child's body, and tell me: I am in love and I am carrying my love in my belly. You come back from the woods and you tell me I'm the one who's crying. Believe me, Nawal, this child does not exist. You're going to forget it.
NAWAL	A person can't forget her belly.
JIHANE	A person can forget.
NAWAL	I won't forget.

JIHANE	Then you will have to choose. Keep this child and this instant, this very instant, you will take off those clothes that don't belong to you and leave this house, leave your family, your village, your mountains, your sky, and your stars, and leave me…
NAWAL	Mother.
JIHANE	Leave me, naked, with your belly and the life it is carrying. Or stay and kneel down, Nawal, kneel down.
NAWAL	Mother.
JIHANE	Take off your clothes or kneel.

> *NAWAL kneels.*

You will stay inside this house, the way this life lies hidden inside you. Elhame will come and take this baby from your belly. She will take it and give it to whoever she wants.

*** *** ***

> *NAWAL (age fifteen) with her grandmother, NAZIRA.*

NAWAL	Now that we're together, everything feels better. Now that we're together, everything feels better. Now that we're together, everything feels better. Now that we're together, everything feels better. Now that we're together, everything feels better.
NAZIRA	Be patient, Nawal. You only have one more month to go.
NAWAL	I should have left, Grandmother, and not knelt, I should have given back my clothes, everything, and left the house, the village, everything.
NAZIRA	Poverty is to blame for all of this, Nawal. There's no beauty in our lives. No beauty. Just the anger of a hard and hurtful life. Signs of hatred on every street corner. No one to speak gently to things. You're right, Nawal, you lived the love you were meant to live, and the child you're going to have will be taken away from you. What is left for you? You can fight poverty, perhaps, or drown in it.

> NAZIRA *is no longer in the room. Someone is knocking on the window.*

WAHAB'S VOICE
Nawal! Nawal, it's me.

NAWAL Wahab!

WAHAB'S VOICE
Listen to me, Nawal. I don't have much time. At dawn, they're taking me away, far from here and far from you. I've just come back from the rock where the white trees stand. I said goodbye to the scene of my childhood, and my childhood is full of you, Nawal. Tonight, childhood is a knife they've stuck in my throat. Now I'll always have the taste of your blood in my mouth. I wanted to tell you that. I wanted to tell you that tonight, my heart is full of love, it's going to explode. Everyone keeps telling me I love you too much. But I don't know what that means, to love too much, I don't know what it means to be far from you, what it means not to have you with me. I will have to learn to live without you. Now I understand what you were trying to say when you asked: "Where will we be in fifty years?" I don't know. But wherever I am, you will be there. We dreamed of seeing the ocean together. Listen, Nawal, I'm telling you, listen, the day I see the ocean, the word ocean will explode in your head, it will explode and you will burst into tears because you will know that I'm thinking of you. No matter where I am, we will be together. There is nothing more beautiful than being together.

NAWAL I hear you, Wahab.

WAHAB'S VOICE
Don't dry your tears, because I won't dry mine from now to dawn, and when you give birth to our child, tell him how much I love him, how much I love you. Tell him.

NAWAL I'll tell him, I promise you I'll tell him. For you and for me, I'll tell him. I'll whisper in his ear: "No matter what happens, I will always love you." I'll tell him for you and for me. And I'll go back to the rock where the white trees stand and I'll say goodbye to childhood, too. And my childhood will be a knife stuck in my throat.

NAWAL is alone.

***

Night. NAWAL is giving birth.

NAZIRA, JIHANE, and ELHAME.

ELHAME hands the baby to NAWAL (age fifteen).

ELHAME   It's a boy.

NAWAL   No matter what happens, I will always love you! No matter what happens, I will always love you.

NAWAL slips a clown nose into the baby's swaddling clothes. They take the child away from her.

ELHAME   I'm going south. I'll take the child with me.

NAZIRA   I feel like I'm a thousand years old. Days go by and months are gone. The sun rises and sets. The seasons go by. Nawal no longer speaks, she wanders about in silence. Her belly is gone and I feel the ancient call of the earth. Too much pain has been with me for too long. Take me to my bed. As winter ends, I hear death's footsteps in the rushing water of the streams.

NAZIRA is bedridden.

***

NAZIRA is dying.

NAZIRA   Nawal!

NAWAL (age sixteen) comes running.

Take my hand, Nawal!

There are things we want to say at the moment of our death. Things we'd like to tell the people we have loved, who have loved us... to help them one last time... to tell them one last time... to prepare them for happiness...! A year ago, you gave birth to a child, and ever since, you've been walking around in a haze. Don't fall, Nawal, don't say yes. Say no. Refuse. Your love is gone, your child is gone. He turned one. Just a few days ago. Don't accept it, Nawal, never accept it. But if you're going to refuse, you have to know how to talk. So be courageous and work hard, sweet Nawal! Listen to what an old woman on her deathbed has to say to you: learn to read, learn to write, learn to count, learn to speak. Learn. It's your only hope if you don't want to turn out like us. Promise me you will.

NAWAL I promise you I will.

NAZIRA In two days, they will bury me. They'll put me in the ground, facing the sky, and everyone will throw a pail of water on me, but they won't write anything on the stone because no one knows how to write. When you know how to write, Nawal, come back and engrave my name on the stone: Nazira. Engrave my name because I have kept my promises. I'm leaving, Nawal. My time has come. We… our family, the women in our family… are caught in the web of anger. We have been for ages: I was angry at my mother, and your mother is angry at me, just as you are angry at your mother. And your legacy to your daughter will be anger, too. We have to break the thread. So learn. Then leave. Take your youth and any possible happiness and leave the village. You are the bloom of this valley, Nawal. You are its sensuality and its smell. Take them with you and tear yourself away from here, the way we tear ourselves from our mother's womb. Learn to read, write, count, and speak. Learn to think. Nawal. Learn.

NAZIRA dies.

She is lifted from her bed.

She is lowered into a hole.

Everyone throws a pail of water on her body.

It is nighttime.

Everyone bows their head in silence.

A cellphone starts ringing.

***

Cemetery. Day.

ALPHONSE LEBEL, JANINE, and SIMON at a graveside.

ALPHONSE LEBEL answers the phone.

ALPHONSE LEBEL

Hello, Alphonse Lebel, Notary.

Yes, I called you. I've been trying to reach you for two hours! What's going on? Nothing. That's the problem. We were supposed to have three pails of water at the graveside, and they're not here. Yes, I'm the one who called for the pails of water.

What do you mean, "What's the problem, there's no problem." There's one big problem. I told you we requested three pails of water and they're not here. We're in the cemetery, where do you think we are, for crying out loud! How thick can you get? We're here for Nawal Marwan's burial.

Three pails of water!

Of course it was understood. Clearly understood. I came myself. I notified everyone: a special burial, we only need three pails of water. It didn't seem that complicated, I even asked the custodian: "Do you want us to bring our own pails of water?" He said "Of course not. We'll prepare them for you. You've got enough on your mind already." So I said fine. But here we are, in the cemetery, and there are no pails of water, and now we've got a lot more on our minds. I mean. This is a burial! Not a bowling party. Honestly! I mean, we're not difficult: no coffin, no tombstone, nothing. The bare minimum. Simple. We're making it very simple, we're only asking for three miserable pails of water, and the cemetery administration can't meet the challenge. Honestly!

What do you mean you're not used to requests for pails of water? We're not asking you to be used to it, we're asking for the pails of water. We're not asking you to reinvent the deal. That's right. Three. No. Not one, three. No, we can't take one and fill it three times. We want three pails of water filled once.

Yes, I'm sure.

Fine, what can I say? Make your calls.

> *He hangs up.*

They'll make some calls.

SIMON   Why are you doing all this?

ALPHONSE LEBEL
All what?

SIMON   All this. The burial. The last wishes. Why are you the one doing all this?

ALPHONSE LEBEL
Because the woman in that hole, face to the ground, the woman I always called Madame Nawal, is my friend. My friend. I don't know if that means something to you, but I never realized how much it meant to me.

> *ALPHONSE LEBEL's cellphone rings.*

> *He answers.*

Hello, Alphonse Lebel, notary.

Yes, so, what's happening?

They were prepared and placed in front of another grave.

Well, that was a mistake.... Nawal Marwan.... Your efficiency is overwhelming.

> *He hangs up.*

> *A man arrives with three pails of water.*

> *He sets them down.*

> *Each one picks up a pail. Empties it into the hole.*

> *NAWAL is buried and they leave without placing a gravestone.*

John Mighton (1957–)

HALF LIFE

3M / 4F

There are few playwriting awards that John Mighton has not won. *Possible Worlds* and *A Short History of Night* (1992) won the Dora, the Chalmers, and the Governor General's Literary Award in the year of publication. In 2005, he won the one hundred thousand dollar Siminovitch Prize for his body of work and a second GG for *Half Life*. His career as a mathematics professor at the University of Toronto inspired the text, *The Myth of Ability*, written to complement JUMP Math, a program he designed for children who have difficulty with math.

Half Life can best be described as elegant as mathematical theory—as are John Mighton's plays in general. The softly controlled tone of these two scenes is representative of Mighton's skilful steps from the humorous to the poignant to the profound.

This is a slow dance between two, experienced lovers, Clara and Patrick. These two meet by accident, apparently for the second time in their lives, in a nursing home. Their fated love affair is prevented by Clara's overly protective son, Donald, who objects to his mother marrying "a womanizer," and by a society that only patronizes its elderly, represented by the well-meaning character, Reverend Hill. Ironically, Donald's objections to his mother's marriage also cut short any relationship he might have had with Anna, Patrick's artistic, compassionate daughter.

TAMMY is getting CLARA ready for bed. She holds up a blue dressing gown.

TAMMY   What do you think? It's your favourite colour.

CLARA   It's beautiful.... Whose is it?

TAMMY   Yours.

CLARA   Is it new?

TAMMY   Yes.

CLARA   I don't remember buying it.

TAMMY   I picked it up this afternoon.... It was on sale.

CLARA   Why did you do that?

TAMMY   So you can look your best.

CLARA   Is my son coming?

TAMMY   No, not this evening.

TAMMY helps CLARA into her dressing gown. REVEREND Hill enters.

REVEREND   Knock, knock. I hope everyone is decent.

CLARA   Hello, Reverend Hill.

REVEREND   Hello, Clara.

TAMMY   *(looking at her watch)* I'm just putting Clara to bed.

REVEREND   I won't stay long. I'd like to sit down if you don't mind. You look beautiful, Clara. How was your bath?

CLARA   I've been scrubbed from top to bottom.

REVEREND   Is that a new dressing gown?

CLARA   Yes. So I can look my best.

REVEREND   Is your son coming this evening?

CLARA   No.

REVEREND He visits you almost every day.

CLARA   I don't know what I did to deserve so much attention.

REVEREND You don't have to do anything to earn the love of your child. You can be a miserable failure in the estimation of the public, but in the eyes of your child you're still the most important person in the world…. Not that you're a miserable failure, Clara.

TAMMY   Have you been drinking?

REVEREND I've just come from Mrs. O'Neill's wake.

> *TAMMY starts straightening CLARA's bed.*

My goodness, Clara, your bed is a mess. Have you been having an affair?

CLARA   I don't believe in sex before marriage.

TAMMY   Then you'll have to get married.

CLARA   Aren't I too old to be married?

TAMMY   Reverend Hill has married dozens of couples older than you.

REVEREND I'm not sure that Clara is ready for marriage quite yet. She would have to ask permission from her son. He has power of attorney.

TAMMY   It's past Clara's bedtime.

REVEREND Yes, I should go. Into the dark, cold night.

> *TAMMY continues to straighten CLARA's bed.*

Watching you make Clara's bed has given me an idea for a sermon.

TAMMY   Don't you ever relax?

REVEREND No. I'm afraid I'm condemned to find a moral in everything.

> *Pause.*

There's only one way to make a bed. The pillow goes at the head. The sheets go under the blankets. And then, inevitably, the blankets and sheets are pulled up to meet the pillow. I'm not sure why, but apparently there's no comparison between order and disorder... there are just so many more ways... I think almost an infinite number of ways... for the world to be a complete and utter mess.

TAMMY   No wonder you're losing your congregation.

PATRICK enters.

REVEREND   Hello, Patrick. What are you doing here? Are you lost?

PATRICK   It's nine o'clock.

REVEREND   Yes. And you're in Clara's room.

PATRICK   We have an appointment.

REVEREND   An appointment? But it's time for you and Clara to go to bed.

PATRICK   That's why I'm here.

REVEREND   Come along, Patrick. I'll take you back to your room.

PATRICK   I'd like to stay.

TAMMY   Why don't we leave them alone?

REVEREND   Do you think that's a good idea?

TAMMY   They're adults.

REVEREND   But the rules of the home are quite strict.

TAMMY   Let them have a little time together.

REVEREND   All right. But I think we should stay, too.

Everyone sits uncomfortably.

Why don't you tell us about the code you broke, Patrick? You must have known Alan Turing?

PATRICK   Yes.

REVEREND   I expect he would have overseen your work. What was he like?

PATRICK   Why do you want to know?

REVEREND One of my hobbies is collecting stories about the war.

PATRICK I'm not a hero.

TAMMY I have a surprise for you, Clara.

> *TAMMY takes a tape of old dance music from the forties and a small tape deck from her bag. She shows CLARA the tape.*

I'm afraid it's a little worn. I hope it doesn't break.

> *TAMMY puts the tape in the deck.*

REVEREND When I like a song I'll play it over and over for three weeks. And then I can't hear it in the same way anymore.

> *TAMMY pushes the play button.*

Oh my… that's lovely. Does that bring back memories, Clara?

CLARA Yes. Do you remember this song, Patrick?

PATRICK Yes. Of course.

CLARA It was my favourite song.

PATRICK Yes. I know.

TAMMY Why don't you ask her to dance, Patrick?

PATRICK I'm not much of a dancer.

TAMMY *(taking PATRICK's hands)* It's easy. You just have to step like this… *(TAMMY begins to dance with PATRICK.)* Pretend I'm your date. That's it… you're getting the hang of it. You look very dashing in your officer's uniform. *(looking at CLARA)* And suddenly, across a crowded room, you catch her eye… the woman you've been waiting for your entire life…. Here, Clara. I'll help you up.

> *TAMMY helps PATRICK hold CLARA.*

You'll have to hold her tight.

> *PATRICK and CLARA dance, with TAMMY supporting them. ANNA enters and watches CLARA and PATRICK dance.*

REVEREND There was a time, a hundred years ago, when people had to wait a long time to hear their favourite song. Sometimes they would wait several years between one performance and another. And sometimes they might only hear a song once.

Pause.

Imagine how well you would listen if you thought you were hearing a song for the last time. All the cares and resentments of your daily life would seem so unimportant. You'd let go of any thoughts that might distract you from the song. You would almost forget who you were.

AGNES enters.

AGNES Would you mind keeping the noise down in here? I'm trying to sleep.

TAMMY turns off the music.

REVEREND *(seeing ANNA)* Yes, I think it's time for everyone to go to bed.

***

ANNA and DONALD sit in the common room of the nursing home.

ANNA Is something the matter? You seem very preoccupied.

DONALD No. I'm fine.

ANNA Is your mother sleeping?

DONALD She wasn't in her room. She must be having a bath.

ANNA looks at her watch.

Where's your father?

ANNA He wasn't in his room either… *(laughing)* Maybe we should try to find our parents.

DONALD Yes.

Pause.

ANNA	My father seems to have taken quite a liking to your mother.
DONALD	Yes.
ANNA	I hope that doesn't bother you. I know your father passed away recently.
DONALD	I'm sure it's not very serious. My mother isn't really herself. Sometimes she thinks my father is still alive and that they're still living in their old house. You might warn your father to be a little cautious. He may be hurt if he gets too attached.
ANNA	My father seems to think he knew your mother during the war.
DONALD	Where was he stationed?
ANNA	Near Toronto. Before he was sent overseas.
DONALD	I don't know how they would have met. My mother lived on a farm near Windsor. She and my father were married a week before he was shipped to Hong Kong. During his imprisonment he lost over forty pounds. He contracted rickets and malaria. And he was beaten mercilessly by the guards. But he wrote in his diary, "We are determined to bear our humiliation without a murmur." My mother didn't receive a letter from him for two years. She didn't know if he was alive or dead. But she never lost hope.
ANNA	They must have been deeply in love.
DONALD	Yes. They were. Their marriage was the most consistent thing in my life.

TAMMY enters. She walks past DONALD and ANNA and is about to exit.

Hello, Tammy. Have you seen my mother?

TAMMY	She's in the basement.
DONALD	What's she doing in the basement?
TAMMY	Dancing.
DONALD	With who?
TAMMY	Patrick.

TAMMY exits.

ANNA	Well, at least they're having fun.
DONALD	I think Tammy is stealing money from my mother.
ANNA	What makes you think she's stealing money?
DONALD	She buys things with my mother's money, but she never keeps the receipts. And everything she buys is twice as expensive as you'd expect.
ANNA	You should tell the director. There may have been other complaints.
DONALD	But my mother loves her. What if they let her go? It's terrible not knowing what kind of a person she is.... I'm a terrible coward.
ANNA	Why do you say that?
DONALD	I spend half of my visits sitting in this chair. I find it hard to see my mother in the condition she's in.
ANNA	But she seems quite healthy.
DONALD	She can tell you which dress she was wearing the day my father came home from war. But not what she did yesterday.

Pause.

Do you remember the saddest day of your life?

ANNA	There've been so many.
DONALD	But if you had to choose.
ANNA	I suppose it was the day my daughter stopped talking out loud when she played.
DONALD	Your life is hardly the stuff great tragedies are made of.
ANNA	Yes, but it was very sad.
DONALD	This happened on a particular day?
ANNA	Yes. And the worst thing is, I think I caused it.
DONALD	How?

ANNA   My daughter and I had just come home from her cousin's fourth birthday party. She said her cousin was so cute because she always did the voices for her dolls and animals when she played. I said, "Just like you," and she looked stunned. It was the first time she was aware that she spoke out loud when she played. After that she always played with her toys in complete silence. I couldn't hear what she was thinking anymore.

           Pause.

DONALD   This summer, at the cottage, I was aware that I was having fun, but my enjoyment was always overshadowed by so many concerns—worries about the future, about my daughter Nina, my work, even worries about the way our activities were effecting the lake—there were huge boathouses springing up everywhere—all part of the relentless development of the north. But looking back, a few weeks later, I cried—I felt the pure joy of watching Nina jump into the water over and over. I remembered the way she and her friends named every dive—"the pencil," "the chair," "the dead man"—even though every dive was essentially the same, but the way they laughed, the way they shouted out the names, the anticipation... it was so simple... they will never be happier—I cried for that, because it was so simple and so hard to reproduce—because it would never happen again.... People should be put to death at age ten.... What purpose does growing old serve?

ANNA   Maybe the purpose of life isn't ultimately to be happy or to suffer, but to do both at the same time. Children can never experience the incredible bittersweetness of joy and pain at the same time, of life lived in retrospect, the awareness of things passing—for that you need memory—you need to grow old.

           Pause.

           My father would like to marry your mother.

DONALD   You're not serious are you?

ANNA   I think it's something we should consider.

Andrew Moodie (1967–)

THE REAL McCOY

5M / 2F

One of a growing number of young, award-winning playwrights born in the 1960s, Andrew Moodie received a Chalmers Canadian Play Award for his first play, *Riot*, in 1996. Since that premiere at Factory Theatre in Toronto, Moodie has staged his work at the Blyth Festival, Montreal's Black Theatre Workshop, Ottawa's Great Canadian Theatre Company and the National Arts Centre, and Theatre Passe Muraille in Toronto. In this short span, Moodie has also accumulated an impressive list of acting and directing credits in theatre, film, and television. Lise Ann Johnson, Artistic Director of GCTC, wrote for a recent staging of *The Real McCoy* that she is "astounded by Andrew's ability to take larger political questions and distill them in taut human drama infused with a large dose of comic relief."

The Real McCoy, then, takes the "larger political issue" of how an engineering genius, in spite of his strong, inner resolve, was eventually driven mad by the institutionalized racism of the nineteenth century. Even placed in the more comprehensible contexts of a father/son conflict and later, family life, McCoy's human drama is fraught by tragedy. By pitting his protagonist, McCoy, against businessmen who desire his lucrative inventions but run from associating with the man because of his race, Moodie creates a primary dramatic tension, which is tightly underscored by McCoy's life of personal tragedy. The central theme of the play is best expressed by Elijah McCoy's memorable argument, filled with the imagery of his profession, to his immediate detractors, and toward his society in general for refusing to acknowledge his genius without prejudice: "Has it ever occurred to you, that all the evils in this country, the hatred and ignorance, bitterness and greed, are inefficiencies that corrode the gears of our society, and if not for this, we could truly be the greatest nation the earth has ever seen." As true then as today.

It is not by accident that Moodie has chosen the narrative structure (and received some undeserved criticism from one Ottawa reviewer as a result).[1] The powerful figure of Elijah McCoy acts as the narrator of his own life. Such a structure is an acknowledgement of personal narratives within nineteenth century African-American literature. Jeannine DeLombard suggests as much in her analysis of *Narrative of the Life of Frederick Douglass, an American Slave*, the 1845 narrative biography of the famous runaway slave and abolitionist. DeLombard also suggests the significance of the eye and the imagery of sight in these narratives; that is, as a slave, the African-American is never allowed a voice (lest he or she be punished or even murdered) but acts only as silent eyewitness to the cruelty of slavery. Sight, without voice, becomes a means of survival in the antebellum South: "Douglass, in a series of witnessing scenes, gradually shifts the metonym of authorship from the vulnerable, corporeal eyeball to the unassailable, immaterial voice, a shift that corresponds with the text's overall progression from slavery to freedom..."[2] This is a second acknowledgement of the political and historical context of Elijah McCoy's life and struggle, as Moodie freely uses throughout the play the imagery of vision to express McCoy's "slavery" to the prejudice of the time. As the "eyewitness to the cruelty of slavery," Moodie's McCoy is robbed of even this final faculty moments before his death in the closing scene of the play.

An outstanding student at home, a young Elijah McCoy is advanced by his teacher for a scholarship to study engineering at the University of Edinburgh under William Rankine, a specialist in steam technology. This series of scenes illustrates this hopeful part of McCoy's life. Of course, he is set upon by fellow students, Smeaton and Kincaid, but quickly manages to win the praise for his genius from Rankine to the dismay of his antagonists.

This excerpt, like the entire play, offers a series of dialogues that are presented without blackout or pause, following one quickly upon the other, Shakespearean style, even though the pacing within each scene may be slower. This excerpt is also representative of the multiple roles of the play. All characters are played by only seven actors, or rather Elijah and six other actors in multiple roles. Here, the same actor playing Smeaton plays Rankine; Nanny Hubbard also plays Mrs. Donaldbain and Sabrina Cohen; Nurse Wilma also plays Harriet Schmidt. Elijah, Young Elijah, George McCoy (Elijah's father) and student Kincaid bring the total to seven actors.

1   Patrick Langston, "Review: The Real McCoy a less-than-filling feast," Ottawa Citizen November 16, 2007.

2   Jeannine DeLombard, "Eye-Witness to the Cruelty: Southern Violence and Northern Testimony in Frederick Douglass's 1845 Narrative," *American Literature* 73.2 (2001) 245–275.

ELIJAH   I seem to recall walking down a hill to the foot of
              Edinburgh Castle...

SMEATON/KINCAID
              ...walk upon England's mountains green...

ELIJAH   There's a cemetery by an ancient church...

YOUNG ELIJAH
              Excuse me...

ELIJAH   The grave of my namesake, my father's masters' forefathers.

SMEATON   Can I help you?

YOUNG ELIJAH
              Yes, I'm looking for the Faculty of Engineering.

KINCAID   Classes don't start till tomorrow.

YOUNG ELIJAH
              Yeah, well, I thought I'd get a head start.

SMEATON   How clever.

KINCAID   Well it's a good thing you found us.

SMEATON   The faculty has been moved.

YOUNG ELIJAH
              Really?

KINCAID   That would have been embarrassing, wouldn't it. Imagine if
              you showed up here without your pigeon papers.

YOUNG ELIJAH
              Pigeon papers?

SMEATON   You won't need this.

              He takes ELIJAH McCoy's pieces of paper.

YOUNG ELIJAH
              But that's the assignment sheet for...

KINCAID   Ten copies of the nine times table. Each on a separate page.

SMEATON   Pigeon papers.

YOUNG ELIJAH
              I beg your pardon?

KINCAID   Well, that was my reaction.

SMEATON   Leslie Smeaton. Pleasure to meet you.

KINCAID   Jonathan Kincaid.

YOUNG ELIJAH
              Elijah McCoy.

KINCAID   A McCoy. Fascinating.

YOUNG ELIJAH
              So…

SMEATON   The new faculty?

YOUNG ELIJAH
              Yes.

SMEATON   I'll draw you a map.

              SMEATON and KINCAID pull YOUNG ELIJAH McCoy
              away. SMEATON hands him a piece of paper, SMEATON
              and KINCAID exit.

ELIJAH   There is a kind of walk that a young man has, when he gets
              it in his head that he is in tune with the whole entire world
              and not a single solitary thing is beyond his comprehension,
              beyond his grasp.

              ELIJAH hands YOUNG ELIJAH a pencil. YOUNG ELIJAH
              writes a letter. As the letter is written, NANNY HUBBARD
              and GEORGE McCoy enter, they move across the stage, they
              grow closer and closer together. By the end, they are holding
              hands.

YOUNG ELIJAH
              Dear Father.

ELIJAH   The world…

NANNY HUBBARD

> *The world…*

YOUNG ELIJAH

> The world is a complete harmony…

NANNY HUBBARD

> *…who's sweetest mysteries…*

ELIJAH   Mysteries.

NANNY HUBBARD

> *…intimate the possibility of a life without suffering, without fear.*

YOUNG ELIJAH

> Where every problem has a solution and every…

ELIJAH   …solution leads man closer and closer to…

NANNY HUBBARD

> *…the true destiny that the creator of all things intended for us.*

YOUNG ELIJAH

> It is our responsibility…

ELIJAH   …our indemnity…

NANNY HUBBARD

> *…to struggle to achieve our true potential.*

YOUNG ELIJAH

> For good, for justice.

NANNY HUBBARD

> *A full and generous love of our fellow man is within our grasp.*

YOUNG ELIJAH

> I can feel it.

ELIJAH   I can feel it.

> *NANNY HUBBARD kisses GEORGE on the cheek.*
> *YOUNG ELIJAH grabs his satchel and runs around town.*
> *Actor number four enters.*

YOUNG ELIJAH

> Excuse me, is this the Faculty of Engineering?

NURSE WILMA

Medicine.

YOUNG ELIJAH

I beg your pardon?

ELIJAH   There are three main founders of the modern science of thermodynamics.

Actor number five enters.

YOUNG ELIJAH

Excuse me, is this the Faculty of...

MRS. DONALDBAIN

Law? Yes it is, please, come in.

ELIJAH   Rudolf Julius Emanuel Clausius.

YOUNG ELIJAH

Excuse me, is...

HARRIET SCHMIDT

No dear.

ELIJAH   Lord William Thomson Kelvin.

YOUNG ELIJAH

Where did they move the Faculty of Engineering?!

SABRINA COHEN

Oh, dear.

Actor number six enters. Stands behind ELIJAH.

ELIJAH   And William John Macquorn Rankine.

WILLIAM RANKINE

God made man an imperfect thing. WE. DON'T. HAVE. THAT. LUXURY. Whatever we design must be perfect and true, or else people die. God does not care if people die. We do.

YOUNG ELIJAH enters, trying to get to his seat, he drops his books on the floor.

YOUNG ELIJAH

I'm sorry. I'm... I'll just...

He quickly picks up his books and hurries to his seat.

WILLIAM RANKINE
You're late.

YOUNG ELIJAH
I am very sorry, I was under the mistaken impression...

WILLIAM RANKINE
No excuses. Sit down. If you're late again, you're out of my class.

YOUNG ELIJAH
It will not happen again.

WILLIAM RANKINE
We'll see about that. As I was saying. Entropy, second law of thermodynamics. The first?

YOUNG ELIJAH
Oh, me? The uh...

KINCAID   The energy within a closed system remains constant.

WILLIAM RANKINE
Very good. These two laws are the left hand and the right hand of God. And they are absolute. Learn them. You're going to spend the rest of your life in defiance of these two laws. With these hands, God pummels the earth. He takes away our loved ones. He shatters the lives of kings. He lays waste to the nameless poverty-stricken masses cowering for a scrap of food left by dogs. Kincaid!

KINCAID   Yes sir.

WILLIAM RANKINE
Energy is related to...

KINCAID   Power over time.

WILLIAM RANKINE
Assignment sheet.

KINCAID   Sir.

WILLIAM RANKINE
McCoy.

YOUNG ELIJAH
Yes?

WILLIAM RANKINE
Where "m" is the mass and "v" is velocity, what is the formula for gravitational potential energy.

YOUNG ELIJAH
Sir, I have to tell you, a practical joke has been played on me, and I… I think you may find it amusing.

WILLIAM RANKINE
I am certain I will not.

NANNY HUBBARD enters with GEORGE, reading a letter to him.

NANNY HUBBARD
As you can imagine from the description, haggis is not one of my favourite meals.

GEORGE McCOY
Sounds fine to me.

NANNY HUBBARD
I have, however, grown fond of a dish called neeps and tatties. I will tell you in my next letter what it consists of, so that for at least a few days you will imagine it to be more exotic than it actually is.

ELIJAH whispers into YOUNG ELIJAH's ear.

GEORGE McCOY
How come he hasn't mentioned school yet?

NANNY HUBBARD
Mr. Rankine and I are getting along like a house on fire.

GEORGE McCOY
That's my boy.

NANNY HUBBARD
I learned from Nanny Hubbard you had to sell part of the land to pay for my tuition.

GEORGE McCOY

Now, what the hell you go and do that for?

NANNY HUBBARD

Don't be mad at her, I just want to say your belief in me and support is greatly appreciated.

GEORGE McCOY

Now, it doesn't say that.

NANNY HUBBARD

If I could become half the man you are, I would be half the greatest man this world has ever seen.

GEORGE McCOY

All right. That's enough.

NANNY HUBBARD

Yours truly…

GEORGE McCOY

I know who wrote it.

NANNY HUBBARD

What's the matter?

GEORGE McCOY

That boy. That boy.

> *ELIJAH and actor number five bring on a chalkboard with a chalk drawing of a steam engine.*

WILLIAM RANKINE

There cannot be a more beautiful and striking exemplification of the union of science and art than is exhibited in the steam engine.

ELIJAH   Mr. Rankine was offered by the queen a position at Glasgow University, where he would be working with some of the greatest minds of the time on some of the most challenging aspects of steam-engine technology.

WILLIAM RANKINE

And I am offering an apprenticeship to anyone who solves this problem.

> *WILLIAM RANKINE spins the chalkboard. ELIJAH stops*
> *it to reveal the other side. It has the following question. "In*
> *a steam engine the condenser is kept at atmospheric pressure.*
> *How will increasing the pressure of the boiler change the*
> *thermal efficiency of the engine?" KINCAID and ELIJAH*
> *square off with pads of paper and pencils. WILLIAM*
> *RANKINE pulls out a pistol.*

Ready... set... oh crap, how does this thing work. *(KINCAID*
tries to point out how it works. WILLIAM RANKINE pulls it
away suddenly.) Never mind. Ready, set, GO!

ELIJAH   You can do it, relax.

YOUNG ELIJAH
Okay, it was Papin who said air exerts pressure, so therefore
a vacuum can do work.

ELIJAH   No no, there are two kinds of entropy, remember?

YOUNG ELIJAH
The conversion of heat into work...

ELIJAH   ...and the transfer of heat from high to low temperature.

YOUNG ELIJAH
Why the hell is Kincaid looking over at me like that for?

ELIJAH   Pay attention to the problem, not him.

YOUNG ELIJAH
Now the value is too high. Thomas Newcomen made that
mistake and Rankine knows it!

ELIJAH   Relax.

YOUNG ELIJAH
But...

ELIJAH   The answer is there. You'll see it.

YOUNG ELIJAH
But...

ELIJAH   You will see it.

WILLIAM RANKINE
Time's up. Mr. McCoy!

YOUNG ELIJAH
Done!

WILLIAM RANKINE
Mr. Kincaid?

KINCAID Thermal efficiency is equal to atmospheric pressure over frictional loss, times engine mass to the power of boiler volume, minus piston volume.

WILLIAM RANKINE
Very clever.

KINCAID Thank you.

WILLIAM RANKINE
And very wrong.

KINCAID I beg your pardon, sir?

WILLIAM RANKINE
McCoy?

KINCAID But sir, I…

WILLIAM RANKINE
Are you still talking, Kincaid?

KINCAID No, sir.

WILLIAM RANKINE
McCoy?

YOUNG ELIJAH
Thermal efficiency is equal to one minus condenser temperature over boiler temperature.

WILLIAM RANKINE
And how did you come up with that?

YOUNG ELIJAH
Oh, it was a doozy, sir. And I have to admit, I was about to make all the same mistakes that were made before by Newcomen, Papin, and Evans. I was about to give up when

suddenly I realized, for heaven's sake, if the pressure of the boiler is raised, the saturation temperature of steam will increase, and therefore the boiler temperature will increase. That is, if you adhere to the theories of one Nicolas Léonard Sadi Carnot, the man whose work you yourself have been trying to substantiate over the past ten years.

WILLIAM RANKINE

Right. Well. Right.

WILLIAM RANKINE exits.

KINCAID   Nicely played.

YOUNG ELIJAH

Thank you.

KINCAID   You are a worthy opponent deserving of my respect.

YOUNG ELIJAH

Yes, I am.

KINCAID   There's an informal get-together at Smeaton's family estate tomorrow night. Would you like to attend?

YOUNG ELIJAH

Some other time.

KINCAID   You sure?

YOUNG ELIJAH

Yes, I am.

KINCAID exits. WILLIAM enters, drunk. As WILLIAM sings, YOUNG ELIJAH tries to slink away, unnoticed.

WILLIAM RANKINE

A party of astronomers went measuring the earth and forty million metres they took to be its girth. Five hundred million inches though, go through from pole to pole, so let's stick to inches, feet, and yards and the good old three foot rule!

WILLIAM RANKINE sees YOUNG ELIJAH.

Pssssst! Boy! Come here!

ELIJAH walks over to WILLIAM RANKINE. WILLIAM RANKINE hands ELIJAH a Scotch and a cigar.

YOUNG ELIJAH

Sir, I don't smoke.

WILLIAM RANKINE

Well you do now! God love you, you bastard, you gave it as good as you got. And I'll tell you something, it is worth all the gold in Persia to see the back end of that snooty upper-crust Kincaid, I'll tell you that. How's the Scotch?

YOUNG ELIJAH

Fine.

WILLIAM RANKINE

You and me. I'll make a master engineer of you, young McCoy. Now, you tell me something.

YOUNG ELIJAH

Yes.

WILLIAM RANKINE

Tell me something.

YOUNG ELIJAH

Yeees.

WILLIAM RANKINE looks around.

WILLIAM RANKINE

I want you to listen to the question that I am about to ask you and I want you to answer honestly, do you understand?

YOUNG ELIJAH

I understand.

WILLIAM RANKINE

Do you believe… that it is possible to send a man to the moon?

YOUNG ELIJAH

I… wow. Uhm. I suppose… I…

WILLIAM RANKINE

Listen to me. It will happen. One day. I'm telling you. This universe… we are going to unlock the secrets of this universe. We are going to pry loose the hands of God, you and me.

YOUNG ELIJAH

Cheers.

To the heavens.

WILLIAM RANKINE

You hear that, you bastard! You son of a bitch! You have no idea what you have unleashed onto the cosmos! You son of a bitch.

SCENE BIBLIOGRAPHY

Banks, Catherine. *Bone Cage*. Toronto: Playwrights Canada Press, 2008, p. 64–73.

Bouchard, Michel Marc. *Lilies*, transl. Linda Gaboriau. Toronto: Coach House Books, 1990, p. 30–6.

Chafe, Robert. *Two Plays*. Toronto: Playwrights Canada Press, 2004, p. 97–102.

Findley, Timothy. *Elizabeth Rex*. Scarborough: HarperCollins, 2003, p. 52–9.

Fréchette, Carole. *Carole Fréchette: Three Plays*. transl. John Murrell. Toronto: Playwrights Canada Press, 2003, p. 80–3.

Kerr, Kevin. *Unity (1918)*. Vancouver: Talonbooks, 2002, p. 120–4.

MacDonald, Ann-Marie. *Goodnight Desdemona (Good Morning Juliet)*. Toronto: Coach House Books, 1990, p. 29–34.

MacIvor, Daniel. *I Still Love You: Five Plays by Daniel MacIvor*. Toronto: Playwrights Canada Press, 2006, p. 15–23.

MacLeod, Joan. *Amigo's Blue Guitar*. Winnipeg: Blizzard, 1990, p. 50–3.

Massicotte, Stephen. *Mary's Wedding*. Toronto: Playwrights Canada Press, 2002, p. 59–66.

Mighton, John. *Half Life*. Toronto: Playwrights Canada Press, 2005, p. 50–60.

Moodie, Andrew. *The Real McCoy*. Toronto: Playwrights Canada Press, 2006, p. 23–34.

Mouawad, Wajdi. *Scorched*, transl. by Linda Gaboriau.

Murphy, Colleen. *The December Man (L'homme de décembre)*. Toronto: Playwrights Canada Press, 2007, p. 37–43.

Panych, Morris. *Girl in the Goldfish Bowl*. Vancouver: Talonbooks, 2003, p. 16–30.

Pollock, Sharon. *Sharon Pollock, Three Plays*. Toronto: Playwrights Canada Press, 2003, p. 210–19.

Sears, Djanet. *Harlem Duet*. Winnipeg: Scirocco Drama, 1997, p. 53–9.

Sherman, Jason. *Three in the Back, Two in the Head*. Toronto: Playwrights Canada Press, 1994, p. 61–66.

Stetson, Kent. *The Harps of God*. Toronto: Playwrights Canada Press, 2001, p. 9–15.

Stratton, Allan. *The Phoenix Lottery*. Toronto: Playwrights Canada Press, 2001, p. 58–68.

Thiessen, Vern. *Vimy*. Toronto: Playwrights Canada Press, 2007, p. 32–6.

Thompson, Judith. *Perfect Pie*. Toronto: Playwrights Canada Press, 1999, p. 29–37.

Wagner, Colleen. *The Monument*. Toronto: Playwrights Canada Press, 1993, p. 34–43.

SELECTED BIOGRAPHIC SOURCES

Benson, Eugene, and L.W. Conolly. *The Oxford Companion to Canadian Theatre.* Toronto: Oxford University Press, 1989.

Canada Council for the Arts, http://www.canadacouncil.ca/theatre/

Canadian Theatre Encyclopedia, http://www.canadiantheatre.com/

Library and Archives Canada, http://www.collectionscanada.gc.ca

Theatre Museum Canada, http://www.theatremuseumcanada.ca/home.asp

BRIAN KENNEDY

Brian Kennedy has an MA in Canadian Studies. Currently, he teaches Drama and English, a career which he has enjoyed for close to thirty years. His students led him to learn more about the history of Canadian theatre. When he's not teaching, Brian tries to improve his hockey skills. This task may take another lifetime. He can be reached at brian_kennedy_2@sympatico.ca.

DATE DUE	RETURNED